THE FEARRINGTON
HOUSE COOKBOOK

THE FEARRINGTON HOUSE COOKBOOK

A Celebration of Food, Flowers and Herbs

JENNY FITCH

With Illustrations by Daneen Nyimicz Griffin
and others

Cover and book design by
Kachergis Book Design, Inc.
Pittsboro, North Carolina

Ventana Press, Inc.
P.O. Box 2468
Chapel Hill, NC 27515
(919) 942-0220

For R.B.,
Keebe, Greg, and Kelley

Contents

Acknowledgments   ix

The Story of Fearrington House   xi

Spring

Spring Menus and Recipes

First Day of Spring   3

Easter Brunch   11

Graduation Dinner   21

Mother's Day Luncheon   31

Bridesmaids' Luncheon   39

The Wedding Reception   47

Spring Projects

Garden Party Topiary for the Wedding   59

The Bride's Bouquet   60

The Honeymoon Basket   62

Candied Violets   63

Summer

Summer Menus and Recipes

Morning Coffee   67

Summer Seafood Dinner   75

August Ice Cream Party   87

Summer Evening with Music   95

Garden Harvest Dinner   105

Labor Day Picnic   115

Summer Projects

Harvesting Herbs   129

Drying Flowers and Weeds for the Fall   132

Herb Vinegars and Oils   135

Herb Butters   136

Pesto Sauce   138

Autumn

Autumn Menus and Recipes

After the Game   141
Pig Pickin' in the Barn   149
In Celebration of Fall   157
Dessert after the Symphony   167
Thanksgiving Day   175
Tea in the Afternoon   187

Autumn Projects

Herb Wreath   195
Bouquet Garni   196
Potpourri   197

Winter

Winter Menus and Recipes

Christmas Dinner with the Family 201
New Year's Eve   213
Winter Get-Together   223
Groundhog Day Lunch   231
Early March Kite Flying   239
End-of-Winter Dinner   249

Winter Projects

Planting the Wildflower Field   259
Forcing Blossoms   260
Planting Paper-whites   261

Index   263

Acknowledgments

To R.B., who is one of the most positive, creative people I know. His patience, indulgence, and encouragement have made this book possible.

To Guy, Cory, Larkin, Margo, Lisa, Ben, Karen, Walter, Robert, Daneen, Joaquin, Jay High, and the staff at Fearrington for their generous contribution of time and talent.

To Keebe, Kelley, and Greg . . . a great group of kids . . . for having to put up with parents whose vocation became their avocation. I hope they will find the unique pleasure that good food, flowers, and herbs can bring.

And to Mama Nell, the best cook I know!

J.F.

Harrington House

The Story of Fearrington House

It all began in 1786 when Jesse Fearrington's great-great-grandfather, William Cole, purchased a 640-acre farm in Chatham County, North Carolina, for approximately $500.

For nearly two centuries the farm was passed from generation to generation of Cole's descendants, who were primarily millers. They used slave labor to raise crops to feed the family as well as to operate a grist mill. Later descendants raised turkeys, produced cotton and tobacco, and finally established the farm as a poultry and dairy business.

In 1974 Fitch Creations, Inc. purchased the Fearrington farm and embarked on the pleasant task of converting the farm area and its surrounding land into a country village. The dairy barn and its silo still dominate the landscape, and cows, now Belted Galloways, still graze in the meadow. The blacksmith shop serves as a post office for the Fearrington community. The farm granary is the location of the Market, which sells home-baked goods, groceries, wine, cheese, and local produce and houses a deli/cafe. The milking barn now houses Jim Pringle's Pottery (some of his work is in the Smithsonian permanent collection), A Stone's Throw (jewelry and stones from throughout the world), and Dovecote (Jenny Fitch's country garden shop). In 1986 an elegant fourteen-room inn opened to house our overnight guests.

The original Cole family home, a one-story structure located deep within the farm, burned to the ground in 1925. A new house nearer Chapel Hill Road was completed in 1927. This two-story frame dwelling is now Fearrington House.

In remodeling to make the house suitable for a restaurant, structural changes were made only when necessary. The room just inside the front door on the right was the living room; today it remains a place where people gather. A new kitchen was built, porches were glassed in, and the old farm office became a private dining room.

Outside the building a knot garden was created from the former parking lot. Formal rose gardens with trellises covered in vines create a focal point for afternoon tea at the Inn. Many of the original trees and shrubs remain and are used for forcing and cutting during the winter and spring months. Perennials and herbs were planted around the trees to make borders that flower all summer long.

Fearrington House opened as a restaurant on May 7, 1980. In 1986 we established our current practice of serving dinner Tuesday through Saturday and a hearty Sunday brunch. In those years we have served thousands of meals as well as hosting wedding receptions, holiday celebrations, and other parties inside or out on the lawn.

By and large, the recipes and flower arrangements in this book are the ones that have found greatest favor over the years at Fearrington House. We hope they bring you pleasure.

Many of the menus in this book contain recipes that are not listed on the menu page but would work equally well in the menu on another occasion. Such recipes are flagged by an asterisk and designated "Extra Recipe."

SPRING

First Day of Spring

Gratin of Leeks and Spring Onions

* * *

Poached Salmon with Cucumber Dill Mayonnaise

Orange Saffron Rice

Sautéed Baby Greens

* * *

Shaker Lemon Pie

Serves 6–8 people

A good rule of thumb to use in poaching the salmon is to cook the fish 5 minutes per inch of thickness. For example, a 3" thick salmon would need to be poached 15 minutes.

Poached Salmon with Cucumber Dill Mayonnaise

1 4-pound fresh salmon, boned and skinned

4 bay leaves

1 lemon, sliced

6–7 sprigs fresh thyme

4 ribs celery, chopped

1 medium-size onion, sliced

¼ teaspoon vegetable oil

1 teaspoon salt

1 teaspoon whole black peppercorns

1 recipe Cucumber Dill Mayonnaise

1. Cut salmon into 6 individual portions. Fill a large roasting pan with 3–4 quarts water, making certain the pan is large enough to hold the salmon. Add bay leaves, lemon, thyme, celery, onion, oil, salt, and peppercorns. Bring to a boil.
2. Poach the salmon about 15 minutes over moderate heat sufficient to keep the stock at a simmer. Cool the salmon in the cooking liquid, drain on absorbent towels, and refrigerate.
3. To serve, garnish each portion with a tablespoon of cucumber dill mayonnaise and pass extra mayonnaise in a separate container.

6 portions

Cucumber Dill Mayonnaise

½ cup cucumbers, finely chopped

salt

1 cup mayonnaise, preferably homemade

½ cup sour cream

3 tablespoons lemon juice

dash Tabasco

4 tablespoons fresh dill, chopped

Peel and slice the cucumbers; salt the slices and let them drain in a colander for about 30 minutes. Pat dry with absorbent towels and finely chop. Blend with the rest of the ingredients and chill for several hours before serving.

6–8 portions

Orange Saffron Rice

a few threads saffron

2½ cups chicken stock

2 tablespoons butter

1 small onion, finely chopped

1½ cups long-grain rice

⅓ cup orange juice

1 orange rind, grated

2 scallions, thinly sliced

2 tablespoons parsley, minced

1. Soak saffron in water for 5 minutes or add to chicken stock.
2. Heat butter in a skillet over moderate heat, add onion, and cook until translucent. Add the rice and cook for 3 minutes or until it looks transparent
3. Bring the chicken stock to a boil, add rice and onion mixture, reduce heat, cover, and simmer for about 18 minutes. Add orange juice, orange rind, scallions, and parsley.

6–8 portions

Butterfly weed and trumpet vine

Spring Flower Arrangement
Butterfly Weed and Trumpet Vine

All the flowers and fruit in this arrangement are in tones of orange. Since the blackberry fruit is not fully ripe, it has a red-orange cast. The top of the grass has the same color. The components used are:

Butterfly weed
Trumpet vine
Blackberry vine with fruit
Wild plum with fruit
Grasses

The trumpet vine and butterfly weed are both conditioned by holding their stems in almost boiling water for a few minutes (wrap the flowerheads loosely in newspaper to keep the steam from damaging the flowers). After hot water treatment the stems are plunged into room-temperature water and left to sit for several hours. This treatment is necessary since the butterfly weed exudes a white milky substance when cut that would contaminate the water holding the rest of the flowers.

Trumpet vine has always been considered a difficult flower to use in floral arrangements because it wilts so easily. The searing process works well on the woody stemmed vine and enables the blossom to stay fresh for several days.

New Potatoes in Their Jackets

"New" potatoes are one of the delicacies of spring and one of the best reasons for having one's own garden.

18 small new potatoes

½ stick butter

2 tablespoons chopped fresh parsley or fresh dill

Cook potatoes in a covered saucepan for about 20 minutes or until fork-tender. Drain. Melt butter and pour over. Sprinkle with fresh herbs.

6 portions

Sautéed Baby Greens

Gather as many types of early spring greens as you can find, looking for differences of color as well as flavor. A good mix is given in the recipe below, but experiment: another mix may be even better. Other possibilities are escarole, romaine, radish greens, Chinese cabbage, endive, and white and lavender kale. About 32 ounces will yield 6 portions.

8 ounces fresh spinach

8–10 ounces fresh beet greens

8 ounces fresh turnip greens

4 ounces watercress

4 ounces Swiss chard

1 tablespoon Balsamic vinegar or red wine vinegar

2 tablespoons chive butter (recipe p. 136)

1 red bell pepper

1. Wash the greens and remove the center rib. Stack the leaves in a bundle, and holding tightly, cut into half-inch ribbons.
2. Begin the cooking process over medium heat in a skillet, using only the liquid that is clinging to the leaves from being washed. After a few minutes, as the greens begin to wilt, remove from the heat and add the chive butter and the Balsamic vinegar.
3. Garnish with red bell pepper strips cut into vertical matchstick pieces.

6 portions

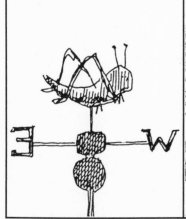

Shaker Lemon Pie

1 recipe double-crust pie dough	½ teaspoon almond extract
2 large lemons	4 eggs, beaten
1¾ cups sugar	1 egg yolk, blended with 1 tablespoon water

1. Preheat oven to 425°.
2. Slice lemons paper thin (with rind), removing seeds.
3. Place lemon slices in a bowl with sugar and almond extract. Toss well and let marinate 2 hours, stirring occasionally.
4. Roll out one-half dough to fit a 9″ pie pan and line the pan. Combine the lemons with the beaten eggs and transfer to the pie shell.
5. Roll out top crust and cover filling. Trim excess dough and flute pie edges. Cut 4 steam vents in the top crust.
6. Bake the pie at 425° for 15 minutes. Turn oven down to 375° and lightly glaze top of pie with egg yolk mixed with water. Bake at 375° until filling is set, slightly puffed, and just starting to brown (30–40 minutes). Cool slightly before cutting. Serve hot, warm, or at room temperature.

6–8 portions

Karen Barker

Double Pie Crust

2¼ cups flour	4 ounces butter
½ teaspoon salt	4 ounces shortening
1 tablespoon sugar	cold water (approximately 6 tablespoons)

1. Combine flour, salt, and sugar in a bowl.
2. Cut in butter and shortening till mixture resembles coarse crumbs.
3. Add cold water, 1 tablespoon at a time, tossing and stirring until mixture starts to clean sides of bowl and dough is formed. Divide dough in half, pat flat, wrap in plastic, and chill several hours before rolling.

Karen Barker

Easter Brunch

Bloody Lucy

*   *   *

Cornmeal Crepes with Smithfield Country Ham
and Leeks

*   *   *

Crabmeat Ramekin

Molded Gazpacho Timbale

Steamed Asparagus and Snow Peas
with Lemon Butter

*   *   *

Raspberry Sorbet in Chocolate Tulip Shells

Serves 6–8 people

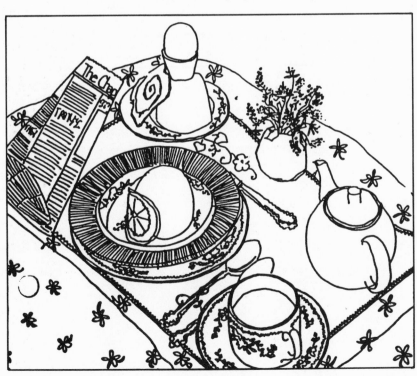

Spring Flower Arrangement

Elderberry,
Queen Anne's Lace,
Palmetto Palm Fronds

Elderberry is in its bloom stage in this arrangement. As the Queen Anne's Lace begins to turn into its cone-shaped seedhead, it makes a nice contrast in shape.

Both elderberry and Queen Anne's Lace are conditioned by being placed in a deep bucket of very hot water as soon as they are cut and then left to sit for several hours as the temperature of the water cools. If this procedure is not followed, the elderberry slowly wilts over the course of the day.

Other equally striking components that might be used in this arrangement are lespadeza, the fern from leafed-out asparagus, and Southern wormwood.

Elderberry, Queen Anne's Lace, palm fronds

Cornmeal Crepes
with Smithfield Country Ham
and Leeks

Cornmeal Crepes (see page 14)

3 leeks, thinly sliced

2 tablespoons butter

4 ounces mushrooms

3 ounces spinach

¼ teaspoon salt, freshly ground pepper

freshly grated nutmeg

4 ounces country ham, minced

Mornay Sauce (see page 14)

1. Trim the leeks and wash under running water to remove any dirt or grit.
2. Melt the butter in a skillet and sauté the thinly sliced leeks over moderate heat until they are crispy tender (about 5 minutes). Add the mushrooms and cook for about 8 minutes until their juices have sweated and evaporated.
3. Wash the spinach and remove the center rib. In a small saucepan, cook the spinach over moderate heat (with the water left clinging to each leaf from being washed) until it wilts. Drain and refresh under cold water. Squeeze by the handful until all the water has been released. Finely chop and add to the mushroom-leek mixture. Add salt, freshly ground pepper, and fresh nutmeg to taste.
4. Blend in the ham and add ¼ cup Mornay sauce, mixing well. Heat through.
5. To serve, place 2–3 tablespoons of the ham-leek mixture in the middle of the cornmeal crepe and roll the crepe. Place two crepes seam side down on each plate and nap with the thinned Mornay sauce.

6 portions

Bloody Lucy

3 cups tomato juice
2¼ cups sauterne
⅓ cup lemon juice
1 lemon, sliced

Mix tomato juice, sauterne, and lemon juice in a pitcher. Divide among 6 stemmed goblets. Add ice and garnish with lemon slices.

6 portions

Cornmeal Crepes

½ cup flour	1¼ cups milk
½ cup cornmeal	2 ounces melted butter
½ teaspoon dried tarragon	2 eggs
½ teaspoon salt	1–2 teaspoons vegetable oil

1. Place flour, cornmeal, tarragon, and salt in a blender or processor fitted with a steel blade.
2. With motor running, pour in milk and butter. Add eggs and blend till smooth.
3. Let mixture rest 30 minutes.
4. Lightly brush a 7″ nonstick omelette or sauté pan with vegetable oil. Heat pan over medium heat until hot. Add ¼ cup batter to pan, tilting to cover surface evenly. Turn crepe when underside is set and lightly browned. Cook on other side 1–2 minutes. Make other crepes in the same manner, stacking and separating them with wax paper. The crepes can be made ahead and frozen if well wrapped.

Yields twelve 7-inch crepes

Karen Barker

Mornay Sauce

2 tablespoons butter	freshly grated nutmeg
2 tablespoons flour	¼ teaspoon salt
1 cup milk	freshly ground white pepper
½ cup gruyère cheese, grated	*optional:* 1–2 tablespoons heavy cream
¼ cup parmesan cheese, grated	

1. Melt the butter in a medium-size saucepan and blend in the flour. Cook for 2 minutes, stirring until the mixture froths and bubbles but is not brown. Remove from the heat and cool before adding the milk to avoid lumping.
2. Heat the milk almost to the boiling point and add all at once to the flour mixture, whisking vigorously.
3. Cook and stir over medium heat until the sauce thickens.
4. Remove from the heat and blend in the grated cheeses and nutmeg. Add the salt and a grinding of white pepper. Remove ¼ cup of the sauce to use as a binder, and thin with heavy cream if necessary.

Yields approximately 1 cup sauce

Crab Ramekin

1 pound crabmeat

½ cup celery, chopped

¼ cup green pepper, chopped

1 tablespoon scallions, chopped

1 tablespoon lemon juice

½ teaspoon salt

⅓ cup mayonnaise

2 tablespoons butter, melted

1 hard-boiled egg, chopped

1 teaspoon dijon mustard

1 teaspoon Worcestershire sauce

dash red pepper

⅔ cup bread crumbs

1 tablespoon cold butter

optional: lemon slices for garnish

1. Preheat oven to 350°.
2. Pick over the crabmeat to remove any cartilage.
3. Combine crab with all the remaining ingredients except the cold butter and bread crumbs. Divide among 4-ounce ramekins and top with bread crumbs (a good-quality white bread sieved through hands). Add a *thin* slice of butter, achieved by pulling a vegetable peeler across *cold* butter, and bake for 7 minutes.

6-8 portions

Spring Flower Arrangement

Building a Mass Arrangement

To build a mass arrangement, first select the plant material and condition it (for cutting and conditioning, see p. 78). Next, soak the oasis until it is heavy and fully saturated and put it in a large tin can. Fill the can to the brim with water and place it in a large basket lined with polyethylene. The soaked oasis and the water combine to give the flowers the greatest possibility of lasting a long time.

At Fearrington House in the spring we use masses of flowering crabapple cut from a tree in the front yard. It is a prized old-fashioned native variety and produces an abundance of pale pink blossoms. There are daffodils by the grape arbor, pussy willow on the mound, and huge Bradford pears and forsythia bushes in the far meadow.

Regardless of whether the flowers to be used are tall and spiky, rounded, or sparse and in need of supplementing with greens, there is a single system for building the arrangement.

(continued on p. 17)

Building an arrangement

Molded Gazpacho Timbale

3 envelopes unflavored gelatin

18 ounces tomato juice

⅓ cup red wine vinegar

½ teaspoon salt

dash of Tabasco

1¼ cups tomatoes, peeled, seeded, and diced

1½ cups cucumbers, pared and diced

½ cup red bell pepper, chopped

4 scallions (white and green parts), finely chopped

½ cup celery, chopped

1 tablespoon mixed herbs (parsley,
   tarragon, chives), chopped

1. Soften the gelatin by sprinkling it over 1 cup tomato juice.
   Place over low heat in a saucepan, stirring constantly until the
   gelatin dissolves. Remove from heat and blend in remaining
   tomato juice, vinegar, salt, and Tabasco.
2. Set in refrigerator until mixture is the consistency of unbeaten
   egg white (stir occasionally). Fold in tomato, cucumber, red
   pepper, scallions, celery, and herbs.
3. Pour into a 1½-quart mold that has been rinsed in cold water.
   Refrigerate 6 hours until firm. Unmold just before serving.

6–8 portions

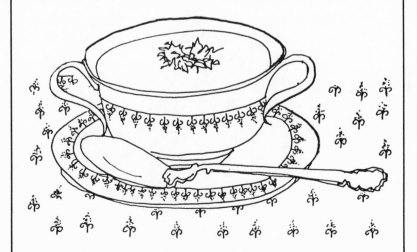

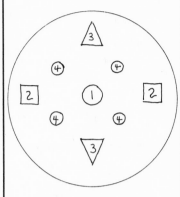

Begin with placement of
the first flower in the center.
Fill in around the center according to the numbers in the
diagram. Angle and force
flowers forward and back-
ward. The placement of the
first nine flowers has now
formed a basic skeletal structure that may be finished and
filled in any manner. This
same technique applies to
both flowers and greenery.

Once the basic shape is
achieved, stand back to view
the arrangement. Fill the va-
cant spots with a variety of
flowers and greens that offer
differences in texture and
shape.

Spring Flower Arrangement

"From the Roadside Ditch"

Nine different kinds of weeds are used for this mass arrangement. All are passing through a stage in their development where they exhibit white color. The weeds are:

Dandelion
Dock
Grass
Lespadeza
Queen Anne's Lace
Sumac flowers
Thistle
White knotweed
Wild onion flower

Since these are pretty tough weeds, no special conditioning is necessary. All are put in room-temperature water as soon as they are cut except for the Queen Anne's Lace. It is put in very hot water and left to sit until the water reaches room temperature.

Steamed Asparagus and Snow Peas with Lemon Butter

12 ounces asparagus

½ pound snow peas

4 ounces butter

2 teaspoons lemon juice

1 teaspoon grated lemon rind

1. Snap the ends of the asparagus, string the snow peas on both sides, and wash and drain the vegetables. Bring a large pot of water to a boil. Cook the asparagus 2–3 minutes, remove from the pan, and refresh under cold running water to set the color. Cook the snow peas for 1 minute, drain, and refresh.

2. Melt the butter in a small saucepan and combine with the lemon juice and rind. Just before serving, drizzle the vegetables with lemon butter. (Lemon juice will turn the vegetables brown if allowed to stand for half an hour or more.)

6 portions

From the roadside ditch

Raspberry Sorbet
in Chocolate Tulip Shells

½ cup sugar

¾ cup water

2 10-ounce packages frozen raspberries

3 tablespoons fresh lemon juice

1 tablespoon raspberry liqueur (Framboise)
or Kirsch

1 recipe Chocolate Tulip Shells

6 tablespoons melba sauce (available at specialty
food stores)

1. Make a simple syrup by simmering the water and sugar together
   until the sugar dissolves. Cool.
2. Purée the raspberries in a blender and push through a strainer to
   remove the seeds.
3. Combine raspberry purée, sugar syrup, lemon juice, and liqueur.
   Freeze 20 minutes.
4. To serve, fill each tulip shell with a scoop of sorbet and top with
   a tablespoon of melba sauce. Garnish with fresh raspberries, if
   available, or fresh violets or mint.

6 portions

The back yard at Fearrington House abounds with violets, which are a sure sign of spring. Inside, they are used in salads, floated in champagne, and candied to use on desserts.

Chocolate Tulip Shells

4 ounces unsalted butter, softened

⅓ cup sugar

3 tablespoons cocoa

2 egg whites

5 tablespoons unbleached flour

2 tablespoons almonds, finely minced

1–2 teaspoons vegetable oil

1. Preheat oven to 400°.
2. Beat the butter and sugar together until pale and fluffy. Add cocoa. Blend in the egg whites quickly, and add the flour and almonds.
3. Butter and flour a baking sheet and draw two circles 4″ in diameter with the tip of a rubber spatula. (Since the tulip cups are to be molded immediately as they come from the oven, it is better to work with small batches.)
4. Spread a heaping tablespoon of batter in the middle of each circle and spread to fill in the drawn area. Bake at 400° for 5–6 minutes.
5. Remove the cookies from the oven and carefully loosen their edges with a spatula. Turn right side down into two 6-ounce oiled custard cups to quickly mold the cookies into the cup shape. Let the cookies sit in the cups for about 1 minute, then remove to a cake rack to crisp. Continue to bake the other cookies two at a time in the same manner.

Yields 6 cookie tulip shells

Graduation Dinner

May Wine

*   *   *

Artichoke-Asparagus Vinaigrette

*   *   *

Boneless Saddle of Veal Stuffed
with Veal Tenderloin

Mushroom Spinach Timbale

Rice with Shallots and Poppy Seeds
Carrots Fines Herbes

*   *   *

Hazelnut Meringue Shells with Chocolate Ice
Cream and Raspberry Sauce

Serves 6 people

Flower Arranging Tip

Flowers That Change Their Direction

Calla lilies *never seem to have straight stems. Arrange them in a straight glass heavy-columned vase and they will bend and twist every way. The next day they will all have straightened by themselves. They are long-lasting cut flowers.*

Snapdragons *always seek the light and the tips always turn. If they are arranged horizontally in a mass arrangement one day, the next day the tips are turned upward.*

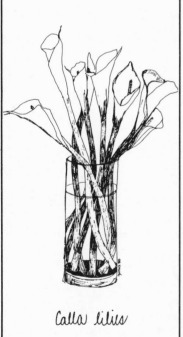

Calla lilies

May Wine

3 sprigs fresh sweet woodruff

1 bottle (750 ml) white wine

6 fresh strawberries

violets or Johnny Jump-ups

1. Pick the woodruff the day before, and put it on a cake rack to dry or crisp it in a slow oven for about 30 minutes. The fragrance of the woodruff develops as it is dried.
2. Steep the wine with the woodruff at least 4–6 hours. Filter through cheesecloth and chill.
3. Place a whole strawberry in each of 6 oversized round bowl wine goblets, and fill each goblet with the wine. Garnish with violets, Johnny Jump-ups, or fresh woodruff sprigs.

6 portions

Champagne may be substituted for half of the wine. To serve 12 people, steep the woodruff in 750 ml wine and add the champagne just before serving. Two other options are steeping 1 sliced lemon in the woodruff/wine mixture before filtering, or adding 2 cups brandy (instead of champagne) once the wine has been filtered.

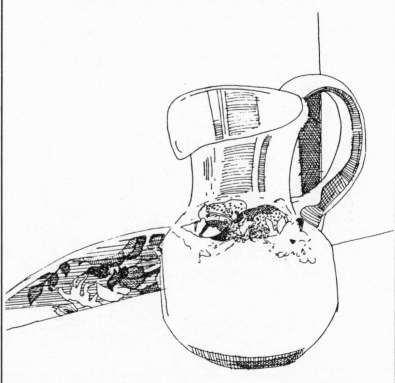

Artichoke-Asparagus Vinaigrette

This recipe brings together several very different components. It is well worth the effort and makes a smashing first course.

6 fresh artichokes

½ fresh lemon

18 asparagus tips

2 leeks, thinly sliced

4 scallions, thinly sliced

½ red bell pepper, thinly sliced

1 tablespoon unsalted butter

1 tablespoon olive oil

3 tablespoons mixed herbs (chives, tarragon, parsley), minced

1 recipe Vinaigrette (p. 33)

Be sure to cook artichokes in an enamel or stainless steel pan. Cooking them in an aluminum pan will turn them gray.

1. Cut the stems and tops from 6 fresh artichokes. Bend the outer leaves of the artichoke and snap each one off at the base. When the purplish thistle is reached, use a sharp knife to cut it away from the base. Trim the base and rub with lemon half.
2. Cook the artichoke hearts in boiling water over moderate heat for about 25 minutes until they can be easily pierced with a fork. Drain them and marinate in about half the vinaigrette, reserving the other half for the asparagus. Chill.
3. Snap the tips from the asparagus in 3″ lengths, reserving the stems for another use. Cook in boiling water 1–2 minutes. Drain and refresh under cold water and set aside.
4. Clean the leeks under running water and thinly slice them along with the scallions (green and white parts) and red pepper. Cook over moderate heat in butter and oil for about 10 minutes until all are soft but not brown.
5. To serve, divide the artichoke hearts among 6 plates, and add the leek-scallion-pepper mixture. Arrange 3 asparagus tips on top and drizzle the vinaigrette mixture over all. Sprinkle with the minced herbs.

6 portions

For an elegant variation, top the artichoke hearts with fresh boiled shrimp and nap with a vinaigrette.

Chicken with Lemon Parsley Sauce

This is an adaptation of a recipe brought back from cooking school in France. Use it as a change in the menu in place of the veal another time.

- 2 lemons
- 6–8 boned chicken breasts
- ½ teaspoon salt, freshly ground white pepper
- 2 tablespoons flour
- 3–4 tablespoons butter
- 3 scallions (green and white parts), minced
- 1 cup white wine
- 2 cups sour cream or crème fraiche
- 3 tablespoons fresh parsley, minced

1. Remove rind from the lemons with a vegetable peeler and scrape off the bitter white pith left on the skin. Poach the strips in boiling water for 2–3 minutes, refresh under cold water, and drain. Cut the strips into thin matchstick pieces and set them aside.

2. Salt and pepper the chicken breasts and dust lightly with flour. Sauté in butter about 15 minutes, turning once. Add the scallions to the pan while the chicken is cooking.

3. Remove the chicken breasts and excess butter from the pan. Add the wine, raise the heat, and scrape the bottom of the pan. Squeeze the two lemons and add the juice to the pan. Cook to slightly reduce. Add the sour cream and whisk until smooth.

(Continued on p. 25)

Boneless Saddle of Veal Stuffed with Veal Tenderloin

This recipe produces excellent results from a simple method of cooking but depends upon a cooperative butcher. It will be worth the effort to fine him.

- ½ saddle of veal, approximately 5 lbs
- 5–7 veal bones
- 1 tablespoon corn oil
- freshly ground white pepper
- 2 16-ounce cans chicken stock
- 1 tablespoon fresh ginger, roughly chopped
- 1 teaspoon garlic, roughly chopped
- 1 tablespoon shallots, roughly chopped
- 1 bottle chardonnay wine
- 2 tablespoons butter, room temperature

1. Have the butcher remove the veal loin and the tenderloin from the bones. Ask to have bones cut into manageable pieces 1–2″ in size.
2. Preheat oven to 450°. Completely trim all fat and silver skin from both pieces of meat. Place reserved bones, fat, and trimmings in a large shallow roasting pan and bake approximately 40 minutes until well browned.
3. Place the loin flat on a countertop. Insert a boning knife horizontally into the center of the loin to make a pocket for the tenderloin approximately 2″ at its opening tapering until it barely pierces the opposite end.
4. Thread kitchen twine through the loin, starting at the small opening and going through the larger opening. Wrap twine securely around the small end of the tenderloin. Pull the tenderloin completely into the loin. Holding the loin firmly, pull the string out (a small amount of tenderloin may break off as it pulls out.)
5. Rub the meat with corn oil and dust lightly with the freshly ground white pepper. Place on a rack in a roasting pan and set aside.
6. Remove the bones from the oven and pour the chicken stock over them. With a wooden spoon, thoroughly incorporate all caramelized drippings in the pan with the stock. Pour the entire ingredients of the roasting pan into a large stockpot. Add the ginger, garlic, and shallots and simmer for 30 minutes.
7. While the chicken stock mixture is simmering, place the chardonnay in a separate saucepan over medium heat and reduce to ⅓ cup.

8. Reduce oven temperature to 400°. Place the roast in the oven and bake for 20–25 minutes until an internal thermometer registers 120° (for a medium-rare roast) when inserted into the center of the roast. Remove from the oven and set aside.

9. Strain the stock into the reduced wine (volume in the sauce-pan should be approximately 1½ cups). Simmer until the sauce thickens slightly. Off the heat, add the butter, stirring until it is thoroughly incorporated into the sauce.

10. Portion the meat to two slices per person. Slice and spoon sauce over top. Serve immediately.

Serves 6 people

Cory Mattson

Return the chicken breasts to the pan to warm through.

4. To serve, nap the chicken breasts with the sauce and sprinkle lemon rind strips and parsley on top.

6–8 portions

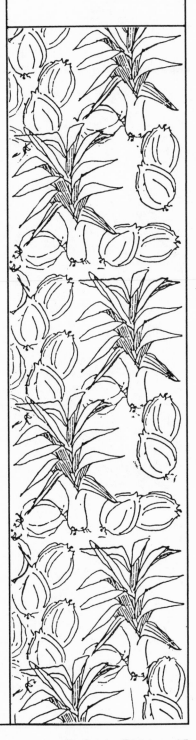

See p. 165 for Baked Vidalia Onion.

Vidalia Onions and Leeks Vinaigrette *

The Vidalia onion is one of the South's special food products. It is grown only in one specific area of Georgia, where the soil conditions must contribute to its unique sweet flavor. The onions are harvested in May and so become a special seasonal treat, allegedly served raw on silver platters as cocktail food in some areas of the South. They are often served as a first course in the summertime at Fearrington House and would fit in the Graduation Dinner menu on another occasion.

2 Vidalia onions

9 leeks

lettuce leaves to line 6 plates

2 fresh tomatoes

2 hard-boiled eggs

2 tablespoons fresh tarragon, minced

1 tablespoon fresh parsley, minced

1 tablespoon fresh chives, minced

1 recipe Vinaigrette (p. 33)

1. Peel the onions and cook covered in a steamer over boiling water for 20-30 minutes until they are fork-tender. Set aside and cool on a wire rack.
2. Trim the leeks to a 4″ length. Slit lengthwise (almost to the base) under running water to remove any dirt. Steam covered over boiling water for 15 minutes until they are just tender. Set aside to cool.
3. To assemble, line the plates with lettuce leaves. Cut the leeks in half lengthwise and put 3 halves on each plate. Cut vertical slices from the Vidalia onions to show a pretty pattern and divide among the plates on top of the leeks.
4. Peel, seed, and chop the tomatoes and arrange as a band across the leeks and onions. Put the eggs through a small mouli grater or sieve, and sprinkle as a garnish on top of the tomatoes along with the fresh herbs. Spoon 2 tablespoons vinaigrette over each plate.

6 portions

* Extra Recipe

Mushroom Spinach Timbale

2 tablespoons butter

¾ cup mushrooms, finely chopped

⅓ cup scallions (green and white parts), minced

2 10-ounce packages spinach, cooked, drained, and squeezed dry

2 tablespoons sherry

1½ cups heavy cream

4 eggs

¼ teaspoon salt, freshly ground white pepper

freshly grated nutmeg

1 cup freshly grated parmesan cheese, or a mixture of gruyère and parmesan according to taste

1. Preheat oven to 325°.
2. Melt the butter in a heavy skillet and sauté the chopped mushrooms and scallions over moderately high heat for about 5 minutes. The mushrooms must sweat and evaporate their juices.
3. Squeeze the spinach in small batches until the water is removed. Chop finely and add to the mushrooms along with the sherry. Set aside.
4. Warm the cream and whisk in the eggs one at a time. Add salt, white pepper, nutmeg, and ½ cup of the cheese mixture, and stir until cheese is melted.
5. Combine the two mixtures and pour into six 4-ounce ramekins that have been buttered lightly, filling them ¾ full. Sprinkle with the remaining cheese. Place on a rack in a large baking pan and fill the pan ⅔ full of hot, but not boiling, water. Bake at 325° for 30–40 minutes. Check during the baking process to make sure that the water simmers around the ramekins but never boils.

6 portions

Variation: The timbale may be cooked in a larger container or even a ring mold. The cooking time may vary depending on the size of the mold, the larger container needing 15–20 minutes longer to bake. During the baking process shake the container: if the middle and the edges move in different directions, continue to bake until all moves back and forth together.

Unmold the ring mold and fill with steamed asparagus spears. Add small pieces of steamed diagonally sliced carrots, and drizzle the inside vegetables with lemon butter.

Rice with Shallots and Poppy Seeds

1 cup long-grain rice

2 cups water

2 tablespoons unsalted butter

⅓ cup shallots (green and white parts), minced

2 tablespoons poppy seeds

1. Bring the water to a boil, add rice, cover, and cook about 18 minutes over moderate heat at a simmer.
2. While rice is cooking, melt the butter in another pan and cook the minced shallots over moderate heat for about 10 minutes until they are soft and translucent, but not brown.
3. To serve, blend the shallots and poppy seeds with the rice.

6 portions

Carrots Fines Herbes

1½ pounds carrots

1 cup water

1 tablespoon sugar

¼ teaspoon salt

3 tablespoons butter, melted

2 tablespoons mixed fresh herbs (parsley, tarragon, chervil, and chives), finely minced

1. Peel the carrots and slice diagonally.
2. In a 2-quart saucepan, bring the carrots to a boil with the water, sugar, and salt. Cover and simmer over moderate heat for about 20 minutes until the carrots are tender and the liquid has evaporated. Cook a lesser amount of time for crispy tender carrots.
3. To serve, toss the carrots with butter and minced herbs.

6 portions

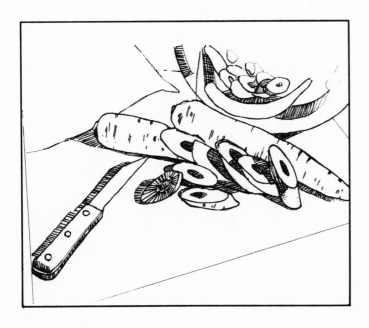

Hazelnut Meringue Shells with Chocolate Ice Cream and Raspberry Sauce

The meringue shells should be made on a bright sunny day when there is low humidity. If made on a rainy day, they weep.

Another time serve the nests with sweetened strawberries and whipped cream.

To make chocolate shells, fold in ⅓ cup cocoa with the sugar and bake as above. Serve with coffee ice cream and a light chocolate sauce.

4 egg whites

pinch of salt

⅛ teaspoon cream of tartar

1 cup sugar

½ cup hazelnuts, toasted and coarsely chopped

1 pint chocolate ice cream

¾ cup raspberry sauce (recipe p. 169)

1. Preheat oven to 225°.
2. Beat the egg whites until they are frothy. Add the salt and cream of tartar and beat until the mixture holds soft peaks. Continue beating, gradually adding the sugar, until the whites hold stiff peaks. Quickly and gently fold in the chopped nuts.
3. To form the shells, use about ½ cup of the mixture for each shell, mounding the meringue on a baking sheet lined with parchment paper. With the back of a spoon, shape into individual nests about 3″ in diameter with an indention in the center.
4. Bake at 225° for 1 hour. Once baking is completed, turn the oven off and let the shells continue to dry for another 30 minutes.
5. To serve, divide the ice cream among the nests and place 1–2 tablespoons raspberry sauce on top.

6–8 portions

Mother's Day Luncheon

Asparagus Vinaigrette

*   *   *

Twice-Baked Cheese Soufflé

Glazed Baby Carrots

Garden Peas with Tarragon Butter

Sausage Pinwheel Biscuits

*   *   *

Strawberry Shortcake

Serves 6 people

Honey Lemon Vinaigrette

Try this delightful dressing on the fresh asparagus spears for a change from the vinaigrette. Its lemony flavor is perfect for asparagus.

2 tablespoons apple cider vinegar

dash white pepper

1 tablespoon honey

1 tablespoon scallions, minced, white part only

juice of one lemon

6 tablespoons corn oil

Whisk together all ingredients until the dressing is emulsified.

Cory Mattson

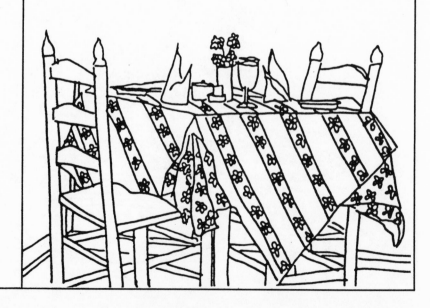

Asparagus Vinaigrette

36 asparagus spears

2 boiled eggs

3 tablespoons mixed herbs (chives, tarragon, chervil, parsley), minced

lettuce leaves to line 6 plates

1 recipe Vinaigrette

½ red bell pepper, minced

1. Snap the ends of the asparagus spears. Wash and drain. Boil for about 2 minutes until the spears can be pierced with a fork but are still crunchy. Drain and refresh with cold water to set the bright green color.
2. Put the eggs through a mouli grater or sieve and set aside.
3. To assemble, line each plate with lettuce and divide the asparagus spears among them. Drizzle with the vinaigrette. Garnish with eggs and red bell pepper, and sprinkle herbs on top.

6 portions

Vinaigrette

In the summertime we make our own vinegars and oils from the Fearrington House herb gardens to use throughout the year. Instructions are on p. 135.

2 tablespoons tarragon vinegar

¼ teaspoon salt

2 teaspoons dijon mustard

6 tablespoons basil-garlic olive oil

freshly ground pepper

In a wooden bowl, stir the salt into the vinegar until it dissolves. Add the mustard and then slowly whisk the olive oil into the mixture by the spoonful. As the mustard absorbs the oil, the dressing becomes thick and emulsified. Add freshly ground pepper to taste.

As a variation, use pimiento cut into one long strip to "tie" the asparagus in a bundle. Omit the egg. Sprinkle the herbs over all.

If country ham is available, mince 1 ounce and use as a garnish.

A vinaigrette is at its best when freshly made. Once one remembers the proportions, it becomes much easier to whisk together the dressing as needed.

For most standard vinaigrettes, substitute red wine vinegar for the tarragon vinegar and proceed with the recipe.

Twice-Baked Cheese Soufflé

The following recipe is a creation of Richard Olney, an American who lives in the South of France. A culinary authority and author well respected by the French, he has graciously given us permission to use his cheese soufflé recipe, a staple of the Sunday Brunch menu at Fearrington House.

1 cup milk	1 cup parmesan cheese, freshly grated
2 tablespoons flour	
½ teaspoon salt, freshly ground white pepper	¼ cup gruyère cheese, grated
freshly grated nutmeg	3 egg yolks
	2 egg whites
4 tablespoons butter	1½ cups heavy cream

1. Preheat oven to 300°.
2. Bring milk to a boil, leave until lukewarm, and pour slowly into the flour, stirring to avoid lumping. Season with salt, pepper, and nutmeg. Cook over medium flame, stirring constantly with a wooden spoon, until thickened. Cool several minutes.
3. Add 2 tablespoons butter, half the grated cheeses, and 3 egg yolks. Beat the egg whites until stiff and fold them in gently but thoroughly.
4. Butter six 4-ounce individual porcelain molds, spoon ⅔ full of the mixture, place them in a larger pan, pour in enough hot but not boiling water to immerse them by two-thirds.
5. Bake at 300° for 15 or 20 minutes or until firm to the touch. Unmold the soufflés carefully, so as not to damage them, one by one onto a large cookie sheet, first running the blade of a knife around the edges to loosen them. This first cooking process may be carried out in advance, if preferred.
6. Raise oven temperature to 350°.
7. Butter a shallow baking dish of the right size to hold all the soufflés placed side by side, but not touching. Sprinkle the bottom with half the remaining cheese, place the soufflés on top, pour in enough cream to immerse them by half, sprinkle the rest of the cheese over the surface, and bake at 350° for another 15 or 20 minutes or until the cream is nearly all absorbed and a light golden gratin has been formed.

6 portions

Glazed Baby Carrots

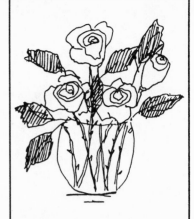

18 baby carrots

½ cup packed brown sugar

2 tablespoons orange juice

1 orange rind, grated

1 tablespoon butter

1. Allow approximately 3 carrots per person. Peel the carrots and leave ½″ of the green top attached.
2. Cook the carrots in a medium-size saucepan or skillet with water for 5–8 minutes until crispy tender. Drain.
3. Mix the sugar, orange juice, and grated orange rind with ¾ cup water. Bring to boil; add the butter. Cook until the liquid is thickened and reduced and the sugar is dissolved.
4. Add the carrots, coat them with the glaze, heat through, and serve.

6 portions

By Mother's Day there is always one rose blooming in the flower border at Fearrington House. This begins a whole season of bloom that stretches all the way to Thanksgiving. During this time there are always enough flowers to take inside to add to a bouquet or make a special arrangement.

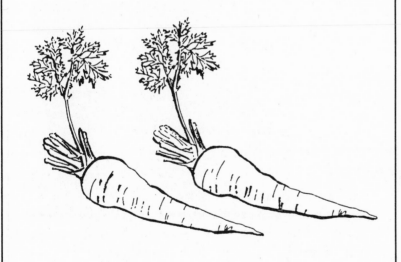

Garden Peas with Tarragon Butter

3 pounds fresh shelled garden peas

1½ teaspoons sugar

¼ teaspoon salt, freshly ground pepper

1 recipe Tarragon Butter (p. 137)

1. In a medium-size saucepan bring water to a rapid boil. Add the peas, sugar, and salt. Bring again to a boil, cut the heat back, and let the peas cook slowly for about 4 minutes.
2. Drain the peas and season with freshly ground pepper. Toss the peas in 2–3 tablespoons of the tarragon butter (cut into small pieces), and pass extra butter with them.

6 portions

Sausage Pinwheel Biscuits

1 pound bulk sausage

1 recipe Angel Biscuit Dough (p. 49)

1 tablespoon butter, melted

1. Preheat oven to 450°.
2. Brown sausage, breaking it apart as it cooks. Drain on absorbent towels.
3. Roll Angel Biscuit dough until it is ½″ thick and approximately 10″ × 15″.
4. Brush the dough with melted butter and spread with the sausage. Shape into a jelly roll and chill. Cut into slices ½″ thick and place them on a lightly greased cookie sheet.
5. Bake at 450° for 10–12 minutes or until golden brown.

Yields approximately 18 biscuits

Strawberry Shortcake

What a perfect spring dessert! It is so plain and honestly good that it is worth the wait for fresh strawberries. The recipe we use is an old-fashioned one and makes approximately 8 shortcakes 3″ in diameter.

3 cups flour

1 tablespoon baking powder

¾ teaspoon salt

¼ cup sugar

3 ounces butter

1 cup milk

1 recipe Fresh Strawberries

½ pint heavy cream, whipped and sweetened

1. Preheat oven to 425°.
2. Work dry ingredients and the butter together in a mixer. Add milk, mix, and check consistency. It should be comparable to a biscuit dough, but slightly more moist.
3. Roll on a lightly floured surface with a minimum of handling until the dough is ¾″ thick. Cut into eight 3″ rounds.
4. Bake at 425° for 15 minutes or until golden brown.
5. To serve, ladle a few strawberries with their juice onto the bottom of a dessert plate. Slice the shortcake, arrange bottom half in the middle of the plate, and ladle more strawberries onto it. Put top half in place so that it leans against the bottom half. Garnish with whipped cream and fresh violets.

8 portions

Fresh Strawberries

1 quart strawberries
½ cup sugar

Empty the strawberries into a large bowl of water and wash them quickly. Drain, remove caps, and slice. Add the sugar and stir from time to time to make certain it is dissolved and the berries have made their own juice.

8 portions

Vary the shortcake by adding the grated rind of one orange to the shortcake recipe. Serve with Grand Marnier Sauce (p. 125) and whipped cream if desired.

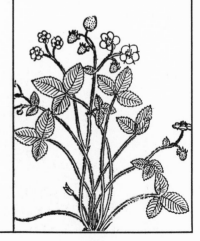

Spring Flower Arrangement

Memorial Day Roses

As rose enthusiasts know, most roses produced in the first bloom period have short stems. This massive-looking bouquet fools the eye, for most of the stems are only 12" – 14". The inside of the container is built up by filling it with mustard jars or coffee cans until the oasis is level or slightly higher than the mouth of the vase. The arrangement is a simple matter of balance.

Memorial Day Roses

Bridesmaids' Luncheon

Berry Patch Champagne

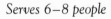

Chilled Cucumber Soup
with Borage Blossoms

* * *

Chicken Salad with Oranges and
Toasted Almonds

Green Beans with Fines Herbes Butter

Baked Cherry Tomatoes
with Toasted Bread Crumbs

* * *

Lemon Frost Pie with Blueberry Sauce

Serves 6–8 people

Chilled Cucumber Soup
with Borage Blossoms

This soup is the result of many years of searching for something better-tasting than puréed raw cucumbers. It needs to be started early in the morning of the day it is to be served, since the base needs to cool before adding heavy cream.

Borage blossoms from the herb garden are used for garnish, not only because of their blue color but also because they taste like cucumbers and thus complement the soup.

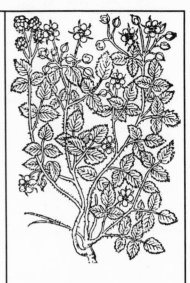

4 ounces butter

2 onions, chopped

2 leeks (white part only), chopped

2 cucumbers, peeled, seeded, and chopped

1 quart fresh chicken stock, or two 14½-ounce cans chicken broth

½ teaspoon salt, freshly ground white pepper

½ cup heavy cream

1 teaspoon dill, minced

½ teaspoon lemon juice

3–5 drops Tabasco

1 cup cucumber, peeled, seeded, and finely chopped

1 lemon rind, cut into matchstick pieces

2 tablespoons sour cream

1 tablespoon parsley, minced

6 borage blossoms

Berry Patch Champagne

½ cup raspberry syrup

1 bottle (750 ml) champagne

12 fresh raspberries, fraises-des-bois, or tiny wild strawberries

A raspberry syrup purchased at a specialty food store may be used, but it is best to make one's own syrup (recipe p. 169).

Put 1–1½ tablespoons fruit syrup in each of 6 champagne flutes. Slowly fill each flute with champagne. Garnish with 2 fresh berries.

6 portions

1. In a stainless steel or enamel kettle melt the butter and cook the onions, leeks, and cucumbers over medium heat for about 10 minutes.
2. Add the chicken stock, salt, and freshly ground pepper. Simmer for about 1 hour. Cool to room temperature and purée in a blender or food processor.
3. Stir in the heavy cream, dill, lemon juice, Tabasco, and finely chopped cucumber. Chill.
4. To serve, garnish each soup bowl with lemon rind, 1 teaspoon sour cream, ½ teaspoon parsley, and a borage blossom.

6 portions

This is an especially colorful tart with red, yellow, and
green. If golden peppers are
not available, substitute red
bell peppers. If you grow your
own bell peppers, simply let
them stay on the vine until
they turn red.

The lemon marmalade is
just the right touch in combining flavors, but orange marmalade can be substituted
if lemon marmalade is un-
available.

Tomatoes

Another time substitute the
fresh tomato tart for a first
course, serve the chicken
salad with asparagus and
snow peas, and omit the
cherry tomato course.

To use fresh tomatoes for
cooking, slip their skins by
dropping first in boiling water
for 15–30 seconds and then
in cold water. The skin bursts
and can easily be peeled.

Deseed the tomatoes by
finding the seed pockets with
your fingers and scraping out
the seeds. This process also
removes the bitterness in the
fruit.

If the tomatoes are drained
after being deseeded, they will
stay in a stable condition and
not weep during the cooking
process.

Peeled, deseeded, chopped
tomatoes look like jewels and
add delectable color to both
cooked and uncooked foods.

Fresh Tomato Tart *

1 recipe Pastry Dough (p. 100)

3 pounds fresh tomatoes

2 tablespoons lemon marmalade

¼ cup basil, shredded

½ golden bell pepper, chopped

optional: 2 ounces black olives, sliced

3 ounces chèvre cheese, crumbled

½ teaspoon salt, freshly ground white pepper

1 tablespoon olive oil

1. Preheat oven to 425°.
2. Roll the pastry to fit a 15½″ × 11″ × 1″ pan, and partially bake
   it at 425° for at least 15 minutes. Remove from the oven and
   drop oven temperature to 375°.
3. Peel, deseed, and drain the tomatoes.
4. Warm the lemon marmalade and brush it over the surface of the
   pie shell.
5. Slice the tomatoes and arrange them in a slightly overlapping
   pattern in the pastry shell. Sprinkle basil, bell pepper, olives,
   and cheese over the top, and season with salt and pepper. Drizzle with olive oil and bake for 20 minutes at 375°.

8 portions

* Extra Recipe

Chicken Salad with Oranges and Toasted Almonds

1 stewing chicken weighing
  4–5 pounds

2 carrots, sliced

1 small onion, sliced

4 sprigs parsley

2 celery ribs

1 cup celery, chopped

1–½ tablespoons lemon juice

½ teaspoon salt, freshly ground
  white pepper

1 cup seedless grape halves

3 medium-size oranges, peeled,
  sectioned, and cut in smaller
  pieces

½ cup mayonnaise

¾ cup slivered almonds,
  browned

1. In a large stockpot cover the chicken with cold water and bring
to a boil. Add sliced carrots and the onion, parsley, and celery
ribs. Cover and simmer gently until tender (about 2 hours). Let
cool in the stock.
2. Remove meat from the bones and chop. Add chopped celery,
lemon juice, salt, pepper, grapes, orange pieces, and mayonnaise. Mix together and chill.
3. Serve with browned almonds on top of each portion.

6 portions

Green Beans with Fines Herbes Butter

1 pound green beans

2 tablespoons fines
  herbes butter
  (recipe p. 136)

4 slices bacon,
  fried and drained

*String the beans from both
ends, wash, and drain. Cook
in rapidly boiling water for
about 3 minutes. Drain and
refresh under cold water to
set the bright green color. To
serve, toss with the herbed
butter and sprinkle with
chopped bacon.*

6 portions

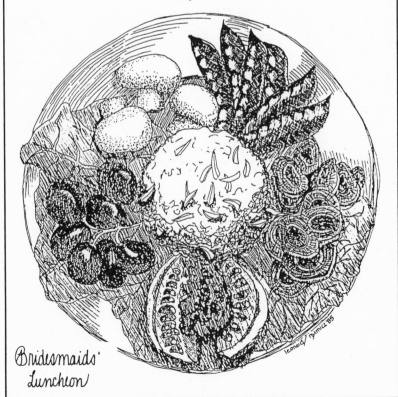

Bridesmaids'
Luncheon

Baked Cherry Tomatoes
with Toasted Bread Crumbs

16 ounces large cherry tomatoes

¼ teaspoon salt, freshly ground white pepper

1 clove garlic, minced

2 shallots, minced

⅓ – ½ cup parsley, chopped

1 lemon rind, grated

⅓ cup bread crumbs

¼ cup olive oil

1. Preheat oven to 400°.
2. Cut the tomatoes in half and gently press out seeds and excess liquid. Let the halves drain upside down for a few minutes, then turn right side up and sprinkle with salt and pepper.
3. Mix together minced garlic and shallots with the parsley, lemon rind, and bread crumbs.
4. Pat the mixture onto the tomatoes, add a few drops of olive oil, and place in a lightly oiled baking dish. Bake at 400° for 10–15 minutes until they are tender but still hold their shape. The bread crumbs should be lightly browned.

6 portions

Lemon Frost Pie with Blueberry Sauce

This pie was made for the first time for my sister-in-law's rehearsal dinner many years ago. It has always been a family favorite, and has since become a favorite on the summer menu at Fearrington House. When it is served, we garnish each slice with scented geranium leaves and white petunias.

1 prebaked 9″ pie shell (recipe p. 100)

2 egg whites

⅔ cup sugar

1 tablespoon lemon rind, grated

¼ cup lemon juice

1 cup heavy cream, whipped

1 recipe Blueberry Sauce

1. In the bowl of an electric mixer, whip whites and sugar until thick and frothy. Slowly add lemon juice combined with the grated lemon rind, and whip until the mixture forms soft peaks. Blend in the whipped cream.
2. Spread into cooled prebaked pie shell and chill or freeze. Serve with blueberry sauce.

6–8 portions

Fresh raspberries with raspberry sauce (p. 169) instead of the blueberry sauce would make the pie seem very elegant and special.

Raspberries are available almost all year long.

Raspberries, strawberries, or blackberries can be substituted for completely different but delightful summer fruit sauces. Berries must first be puréed and then pushed through a sieve to remove seeds. Each sauce will keep in the refrigerator for several weeks.

Blueberry Sauce

⅔ **cup sugar**

1 **tablespoon cornstarch**

pinch of salt

⅔ **cup water**

1 **lemon rind, grated**

2 **cups fresh blueberries**

1. Combine sugar with cornstarch and salt and mix until completely blended, with no lumps. Add water and grated lemon rind. Cook and stir until the mixture comes to a boil and is thick.
2. Add blueberries and let return to boiling point. Remove from the stove and cool. Chill.

Yields approximately 2 cups

The Wedding Reception

Angel Biscuits with Honeycup Mustard and Country Ham

Baked Mushrooms Stuffed with Country Sausage

Garden Vegetables with Dill Chive Sauce

Crab Quiche

Cucumber Sandwiches

Miniature Meringue Shells with Glazed
Strawberries

Fearrington House Fruit Punch

Champagne

Serves 100 people

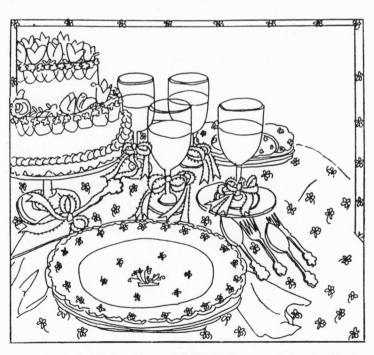

Table arrangement for the bride
Quince, roses, alstroemeria, snapdragons, cedar, boxwoods

Angel Biscuits with Honeycup Mustard and Country Ham

These biscuits have an excellent flavor and are served with every meal at Fearrington House. The addition of yeast makes a biscuit that is almost the consistency of a roll.

10 cups flour

2 tablespoons baking powder

2 teaspoons baking soda

½ cup sugar

2 tablespoons salt

2 cups shortening

2⅓ tablespoons yeast

¼–⅓ tablespoon warm water

4 cups buttermilk

8 ounces honeycup mustard

12–16 ounces country ham, thinly sliced

1. Preheat oven to 450°.
2. Sift flour, baking powder, baking soda, sugar, and salt into a large bowl. Cut the shortening into the mixture quickly with fingertips or a pastry blender until it is the consistency of coarse meal.
3. Dissolve yeast in warm water and make certain it is active before adding it along with the buttermilk to the flour and shortening. Mix all together until smooth. The dough may be refrigerated at this point (place in a greased bowl and cover) or used right away.
4. Knead the dough for 2–3 minutes and roll out on a lightly floured surface to a thickness of ½". Cut the biscuits with a 1¼" cookie cutter and let rise for 30 minutes. Bake for 10 minutes at 450°.
5. To serve, slice each biscuit in half and spread with honeycup mustard. Add a thin slice of country ham and replace the top half of the biscuit.

*Yields approximately 120
miniature biscuits*

Baked Mushrooms
Stuffed with Country Sausage

4 pounds bulk sausage

2 cups fresh parsley, minced

2 cups parmesan cheese, freshly grated

2 cups scallions, minced

8 eggs

2 sticks butter

100 large mushroom caps

1 cup parmesan cheese, freshly grated, for
sprinkling

1. Preheat oven to 400°.
2. In a large skillet, cook the sausage over moderate heat until it is
   broken into small pieces and is no longer pink. Drain on absorbent towels and then mix with parsley, 2 cups parmesan cheese,
   scallions, and lightly beaten eggs. Set aside.
3. Melt the butter in a large skillet and sauté the mushroom caps
   briefly (about 1–2 minutes), rolling them around in the pan.
   Cool.
4. Divide the sausage mixture among the mushroom caps, mounding it slightly. Just before baking, sprinkle each cap with about
   ½ teaspoon parmesan cheese. Bake in a large lightly buttered
   pan at 400° for 10 minutes.

100 portions

Dill Chive Sauce

1 cup mayonnaise, preferably homemade

1 cup sour cream

2 lemons, juiced

1 lime, juiced

3 tablespoons chives, minced

4 tablespoons fresh dill, minced

2 garlic cloves, minced

2 drops Tabasco

½ teaspoon Worcestershire sauce

½ teaspoon salt, freshly ground white pepper

1. Combine all ingredients in the work bowl of a food processor and blend. Chill. Can be done a day ahead.
2. To serve, place the sauce in a hollowed cabbage and arrange on a platter surrounded by a variety of raw and/or blanched vegetables.

Yields approximately 2 cups

making flowers behave

For those flowers that never seem to stay where placed in an arrangement, the following tips may be helpful.

Gerberas, cornflowers, or asters may need to be wired to keep the flowerhead erect. Insert one end of a piece of floral wire into the head from the underside and wrap the other end around the stem two or three times.

Since zinnias sometimes have a heavy head, insert a toothpick from the top of the flower down into the stem.

Roses or tulips may be held in the bud stage or kept from opening by wrapping tape around the flowerhead. This method will keep them at the right stage of development for a short period of time.

To curve a woody branch, slit the stem partway and insert a wedge in that spot.

Daffodil stems may be curved or moved in any direction by first soaking pipe cleaners in water and then carefully inserting them in the hollow stem.

Gladiolas may be coaxed into opening faster by removing the outer tip of the stalk before conditioning. If an individual fully open blossom is desired, blow gently into the flowerhead and work with the fingers.

The quantities given for the crab quiche may easily be cut to yield a family-size entree for a Sunday brunch or a Sunday evening meal. Half a pound of crabmeat will feed 8–10 people (a much more generous amount than the wedding reception portions). The resulting quiche is especially delicious and slightly different.

Crab Quiche

2 prebaked pie shells of Herbed Pie Crust,
   15½″ × 10½″ × 1″

2 egg yolks

2 teaspoons dijon mustard

2 pounds fresh lump crabmeat

8 eggs

2 cups milk

2 cups heavy cream

optional: 2 ounces chèvre cheese, softened

1½ teaspoons salt, freshly ground pepper

freshly grated nutmeg

⅓–½ cup fresh herbs (lemon thyme, parsley, and
   chives), minced

¾ cup green scallions, finely chopped

2 small red bell peppers, finely chopped

4 ounces country ham, shredded

12 ounces Swiss cheese (or gruyère and
   emmenthaler), grated

1 tablespoon butter

1. Preheat oven to 350°.
2. Mix the egg yolks with 1 tablespoon water and paint the prebaked shell with the mixture. Spread mustard over the top and set aside.
3. In small amounts, work crabmeat through your fingers to find and remove small pieces of shell.
4. Beat the eggs with the milk and heavy cream. Add the chèvre cheese and continue to beat until the mixture is smooth. Add the salt, fresh pepper, nutmeg, and herbs.
5. Divide the crabmeat between the two pastry shells. Sprinkle each shell with the scallions, red pepper, and country ham. Pour the milk-cream mixture over each shell and sprinkle with the grated cheese. Dot with thinly shaved pieces of butter and bake at 350° for 35–40 minutes or until custard is set and golden brown. Cut each quiche into 50 small portions.

100 portions

Herbed Pie Crust

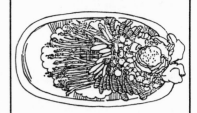

To serve 100 people at a reception, make the quiche in two 15½″ × 10½″ × 1″ pans and cut into squares. For a smaller number of people, line miniature muffin tins with cream cheese pastry and make individual quiches to use for hors d'oeuvres.

2 sticks butter

4 cups unbleached flour

1 teaspoon salt

⅓ cup vegetable shortening

3 tablespoons mixed herbs (thyme, chives, and parsley), minced

1 egg

⅔ cup ice water

1 teaspoon dijon mustard

1. Preheat oven to 400°.
2. Cut the butter into small chunks and add to the flour and salt. Working quickly with your fingers, knead the butter with the flour until the butter is the size of lima beans. Cut the shortening into the mixture and work until all resembles coarse meal. Add the minced herbs.
3. In a separate container mix the egg, ice water, and mustard and combine with the flour-shortening mixture. Toss with two forks until the ingredients are moistened and may be gathered into a ball. Wrap in wax paper and chill at least 1 hour.
4. Divide the dough in half and roll one half on a lightly floured surface into a rectangular shape to fit a 15½″ × 10½″ × 1″ baking pan. Transfer to the pan and roll the edges to fit. Lightly dock the surface. Cover with wax paper and fill with pie weights or dried beans pushed against the edges to keep the pastry from shrinking.
5. Bake at 400° for 15–18 minutes. It is imperative that the crusts be fully baked, since the ingredients for the quiche have a lot of moisture. After 10 minutes remove the wax paper and weights. Return the shell to the oven and brown.

Yields two crusts 15½″ × 10½″ × 1″

All-Purpose Pastry

This pastry made without herbs makes an excellent all-purpose pie crust. The presence of the butter makes a crisp pastry.

The following recipe makes a double crust. Cut the quantities in half for a single crust.

2 cups unbleached flour

1 stick butter

3 tablespoons vegetable shortening

½ teaspoon salt

½ egg, beaten

5–6 tablespoons ice water

Follow steps 2 and 3 of the Herbed Pie Crust recipe for mixing and chilling.

Cheese Pastry

Mix ½–¾ cup grated cheddar (preferably white cheddar) into the All-Purpose Pastry ingredients along with the flour and salt. To prebake, place dried beans in the shell on wax paper and bake at 400° for about 12 minutes.

Cucumber Sandwiches

Cucumber sandwiches for tea or a wedding reception are a Southern tradition. We serve them on homemade tomato bread baked in a shaped tube and cut into interesting shapes such as hearts and clovers. At a home reception, a good-quality white bread will yield the same results.

2 tablespoons Worcestershire sauce

¼ cup fresh dill, minced, or 1⅓ tablespoons dried

2 drops Tabasco

3 tablespoons lemon juice

¼ teaspoon salt

3 scallions, minced

1 clove garlic, minced

1 pound cream cheese

2 loaves white bread
(at least 25 slices each loaf)

6–8 cucumbers, thinly sliced

2 bunches dill for garnish

1. Combine the first seven ingredients in the work bowl of a food processor. Add the cheese in small amounts and blend.
2. Refrigerate for 20 minutes in order to get a better spreading consistency.
3. To serve, cut the bread into shapes, spread a thin layer of the sauce on the bread, top with a thin slice of cucumber (unpeeled), and garnish with a fresh sprig of dill.

Yields 100 sandwiches

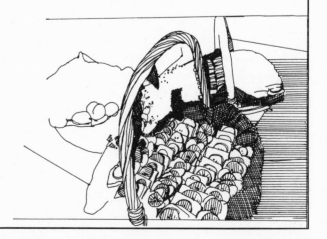

Miniature Meringue Shells with Glazed Strawberries

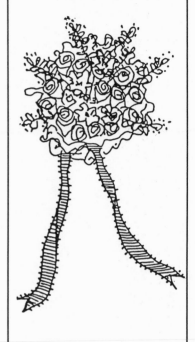

Glazed strawberries make a special after-dinner treat when just a taste of something sweet is wanted.

These meringue shells add an elegant and decidedly Southern touch to a wedding reception. Remember, however, that they must be made on a sunny day or they weep.

> 8 egg whites
>
> 2 cups sugar (for meringue)
>
> ¼ teaspoon cream of tartar
>
> ⅛ teaspoon salt
>
> *optional:* 1 cup hazelnuts,
>   toasted and coarsely chopped
>
> 100 strawberries
>
> 2 cups sugar (for glaze)
>
> ½ cup water

1. Follow the recipe on p. 30 in making the meringues, but divide the mixture into about 100 shells 1″ in diameter. Bake at 225° for one hour, turn oven off, and let dry for 30 minutes.
2. Glaze the strawberries in water-sugar syrup consisting of 2 cups sugar and ½ cup water. Bring to a boil and insert a candy thermometer. Once 265° is reached, lower the heat to keep the glaze in a liquid state. Dip the strawberries into the glaze one by one and set them on a cake rack to harden.
3. Just before serving, top each meringue shell with a glazed strawberry.

100 portions

The punch may be frozen or used as a base for champagne punch or vodka punch.

An ice mold with ferns and miniature roses makes a nice addition to the punch.

Fearrington House Fruit Punch

8 cups freshly squeezed orange juice

1 cup fresh raspberries

4 cups water

2 cups sugar

2 quarts soda water

2 quarts ginger ale

2 46-ounce cans pineapple juice

1 46-ounce can grapefruit juice

1. Put freshly squeezed orange juice through a strainer to remove pulp. Press raspberries through a sieve to remove seeds.
2. Make a simple syrup by combining sugar and water over heat and boiling until sugar is dissolved.
3. Combine all ingredients and chill.

100 portions

Spring Projects

1. Garden Party Topiary for the Wedding

2. The Bride's Bouquet

3. The Honeymoon Basket

4. Candied Violets

Wedding topiary

Garden Party Topiary for the Wedding

This arrangement is prepared specifically for a wedding. It marks the spot where the bride and groom stand at an outdoor reception. Materials needed:

1 plastic flowerpot

1 5-pound box plaster of paris

1 closet pole cut 32"

2 10" wire baskets

2 blocks oasis

5 green twist'em ties or green wire

½ bushel of mulch

1 large terra cotta pot

leaves and flowers

Mix the plaster of paris and pour into the plastic flowerpot. When it is almost set, insert the closet pole, which should be either painted or covered with moss. Let dry 2–3 hours.

Using a square piece of plywood cut 2" × 2", screw one wire basket half onto the pole. Put two blocks of soaked oasis into the basket. Invert the other wire basket on top, and secure it in place with the twist'em ties.

Place the plastic flowerpot inside the terra cotta pot. Fill the terra cotta pot with mulch until the level is ½" below the rim.

Cover the completed ball with boxwood, salau (lemon leaves), or ligustrum. Insert the flowers directly in the oasis until a desired pattern is achieved. Baby's breath makes a nice filler.

Tie ribbons and a bow at the base of the arrangement on the pole, leaving enough length of streamers to billow in the breeze.

The Bride's Bouquet

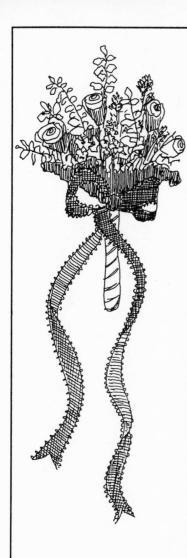

Since Fearrington House is located in the country, we find it appropriate to use wildflowers, herbs, and flowers from blooming shrubs and trees in our bridal bouquets, or a combination of flowers from the florist plus native ones.

Materials needed for the bouquet:

Green floral wire	Scissors
Green floral tape	Satin ribbon, ½″ wide
Needlenose pliers	Conditioned flowers,
Clippers	ferns, herbs

A bouquet is shaped as it is being held in the hand. Begin by gathering 3–5 pieces of fern. Overlap the pieces, letting the middle one extend beyond the others to form a slightly oval shape. This is the base of the bouquet. Foliage should be stripped from the part that will be held by hand.

Add flowers and herbs with different shapes and textures. Remove thorns from roses and strip foliage from the "handle" part. Continue to make additions of rosemary and cascading sprays of ivy.

As the desired effect is achieved, wrap the "handle" first with green floral wire, securing the wire tightly in place with the pliers. Next wrap with green floral tape. Begin covering with satin ribbon at the point where flowers and stems meet. Leave an extra length of ribbon free so that the bouquet can be wrapped to the end and back to the starting point, where it is tied.

Secure the bow in place and add extra streamers that will be free-floating. Tie knots in the ends of the ribbons and cut each in an inverted notch.

List the flowers used and their significance to the wedding on a folding card, and attach the card to the arrangement.

Flowers for the Bride's Bouquet

Azalea	Temperance
Basil	Symbolizes the quickening of love
Dogwood	Durability
Fern	Sincerity
Ivy	Friendship, fidelity, marriage
Lemon balm	Longevity
Lily of the valley	Return of happiness
Marjoram	Youth, beauty, happiness
Mint	Rejoicing
Rosemary	Remembrance. An emblem of loyalty and friendship, symbolizing the lastingness of love
Sage	Esteem
Tansy	Immortality
Thyme	Grace and elegance
Violet	Faithfulness
White daisy	Innocence

The Honeymoon Basket

Materials needed:

> 1 basket, 12″ × 8″ × 7″
>
> ¾ yard fabric 45″ wide
>
> 2 champagne flutes
>
> 12 inches grosgrain ribbon
>
> 6 small silk flowers
>
> 3 corsage boxes, 6½″ × 4½″ × 3½″
> (available from florists' supply stores)
>
> 4 clear plastic containers with lids,
> 3″ in diameter
>
> food from reception
>
> 1 bottle (750 ml) champagne

Cut the fabric with pinking shears. The first piece should measure 27″ × 22″; this will line the bottom and sides of the basket. Napkins are cut 8″ × 8″. The top cover should be 19″ × 23″.

Tie the silk flowers onto the champagne flutes with the ribbon and stuff the napkin inside.

Line the bottom of the basket. Gather foods from the reception and put them into small plastic containers with covers or wrap them in tinfoil; divide them among the corsage boxes. Arrange champagne and flutes. Cover with the top piece and have the basket available for the bride and groom to carry with them as they leave the reception.

Honeymoon basket

Candied Violets

Crystallized violets have been used as garnishes for desserts since Colonial times. Of the two recipes, the first is the simpler, yielding violets that may be refrigerated and used for a few days. The second is a continuation of the first and allows the blossoms to be used and stored indefinitely in airtight containers.

Colonial Candied Violets

2 ounces gum arabic powder
(available at the pharmacy)

1 cup water

1 cup granulated sugar

Combine the gum arabic powder with water in the top of a double boiler and stir until the gum arabic is dissolved. Cool to room temperature.

Dip the violets in the cooled solution, making certain all surfaces are coated, and roll in the sugar. Set aside to dry.

Candied Violets

2 ounces gum arabic powder

2 cups water

3 cups sugar

2 tablespoons white corn syrup

Combine the gum arabic with 1 cup water in the top of a double boiler and stir until the gum arabic is dissolved. Cool to room temperature.

Stick a toothpick into the base of a clean violet. Dip each violet in the cooled solution, making certain all surfaces are coated. Cover a styrofoam block with wax paper and stick the gummed violet toothpick upright into it to dry for 2 hours or so.

Prepare a simple syrup by combining 2 cups sugar with 1 cup water and the corn syrup. Cook until the mixture reaches the soft ball stage on a candy thermometer (234°). Cool the syrup until the bottom of the pan may be comfortably held.

Dip the blossoms into the cooled syrup and again make certain all the surfaces are coated. Roll the violets in syrup and stick in a styrofoam block to dry for about 15 minutes. When all the blossoms have been syrup-coated, remove them from their toothpicks and place them in a shallow pan that has been covered with the remaining sugar. Carefully sprinkle sugar over the violets and let them dry overnight in the pan. Store in airtight containers.

SUMMER

Morning Coffee

Orange-Tomato Juice

Fresh Fruit in a Watermelon Basket

Herbed Cheese in a Braided Bread Ring

Orange Date Cake with Whipped Cream and
Candied Violets

Macaroons

Cheese Wafers with Pecans

Miniature Bran Muffins

Coffee Punch

Serves 12–15 people

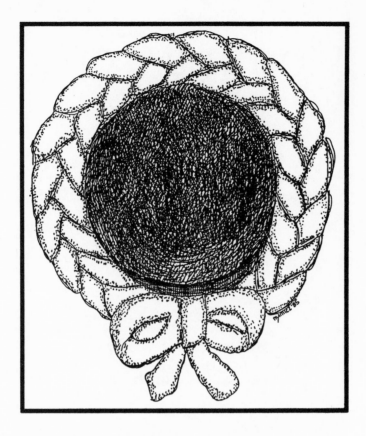

Braided bread ring around inverted cake pan

Herbed Cheese in a Braided Bread Ring

12 ounces small curd cottage cheese, drained

8 ounces cream cheese, softened

2 tablespoons sour cream

1 tablespoon heavy cream

¼–⅓ cup mixed herbs (basil, tarragon, chives, thyme, and parsley), minced

2 cloves garlic, minced

2 scallions, minced

¼ teaspoon salt

¼ teaspoon freshly ground white pepper

1 recipe Braided Bread Ring

1. Work the cottage cheese in the bowl of a food processor until it is smooth. Add cream cheese, sour cream, and heavy cream and continue to process until the mixture is smooth. Blend the herbs, garlic, scallions, salt, and pepper with the cheeses. Do not overwork or the cheese will become thinned.
2. Spread the mixture in a large shallow flat pan, cover, and refrigerate for 24 hours to allow flavors to develop.
3. To serve, mound into the middle of the bread ring. Provide a sharp knife for guests to cut the bread and remove the first slice.

Yields approximately 2 ½ cups

Braided Bread Ring

Use the bread recipe on p. 122, omitting the country ham and herbes de Provence. Cut off 3 pieces and roll them into long ropes about 1½″ in diameter. Oil an 8″ cake pan, invert it onto a baking sheet, and braid 2 ropes of bread together around the outside. Use the third rope to make a bow.

Cover and let rise for about 1 hour. Brush with a glaze made with 1 egg yolk and 2 teaspoons water. Be careful not to let excess glaze collect between the bread and the cake pan or it may keep the bread from rising properly. Bake at 375° for about 35 minutes until golden brown.

Yields one 11″ bread ring

If the cheese mixture is kept cool, it may be cut into shapes with a cookie cutter and used with crackers as an hors d'oeuvre.

Orange-Tomato Juice

For a morning coffee, set out trays of orange-tomato juice (garnished with orange slices) and spiked with a little sugar and lime juice in stemmed wine goblets.

The cake may also be baked in a 9″ × 15″ sheet pan and cut into squares.

Fresh Fruit in a Watermelon Basket

Draw a design for a basket on the watermelon with the tip of a knife and cut accordingly. Remove the flesh of the watermelon with a melon baller and mix with other fruits of different shapes, colors, and textures. Pile the fruit into the basket and garnish with fresh mint or pineapple sage.

Orange Date Cake with Whipped Cream and Candied Violets

4 ounces butter	1 cup dates, chopped
1 cup sugar	2 teaspoons orange rind, grated
2 eggs	1 cup orange juice
2 cups unbleached flour	2 teaspoons lemon juice
1 teaspoon baking soda	1 cup sugar
¼ teaspoon salt	½ pint heavy cream, whipped and sweetened
⅔ cup buttermilk	24 candied violets (see p. 63)
1 cup pecans, chopped	

1. Preheat oven to 350°.
2. In the bowl of an electric mixer, cream the butter and sugar. Add eggs and continue to mix. Remove 2 tablespoons flour; mix with the nuts and dates and set aside. Sift the rest of the dry ingredients together and add alternately with the buttermilk, beginning and ending with the dry ingredients. Fold in pecans, dates, and 1 teaspoon orange rind.
3. Grease and flour a 10″ Bundt cake pan. Pour in batter and bake for 40 minutes at 350°.
4. In a saucepan mix together the orange juice, lemon juice, sugar, and remaining orange rind for the glaze. Cook and stir until sugar is dissolved and the mixture comes to a boil.
5. When the cake is removed from the oven, run a knife around the outside edges of the pan. Prick the top with a fork and pour hot glaze evenly over the entire surface. Let cool. Unmold and serve warm or at room temperature with sweetened whipped cream and candied violets.

12−15 portions

Macaroons

8 ounces almond paste

1 cup superfine sugar

3 egg whites

dash of salt

½ teaspoon vanilla

½ teaspoon almond extract

1. Preheat oven to 300°.
2. In the work bowl of a food processor, blend the almond paste with the sugar. Add the egg whites one at a time, blending well after each addition. The consistency of the dough must be right; it must be neither too stiff nor too runny, and it must be able to hold its shape. Do not use all of the third egg white if the "soft shape" stage has arrived. Add salt, vanilla, and almond extract.
3. Place the mixture in a pastry tube and pipe into rounds on a baking sheet that has been covered with parchment paper. Bake at 300° for 20 minutes.
4. Remove from the oven and slide the whole sheet of parchment onto a damp dish towel. Let the macaroons cool slightly and peel from the paper.

Yields approximately 3 dozen

Flower Arranging Tip

For the one flower that needs to go at the very top of the arrangement but has a stem only half as long as it needs to be, use a test tube purchased from a chemical supply store. Tape the tube to a long dowel stick with green floral tape, fill it with water, insert the flower stem, and put the flower in place.

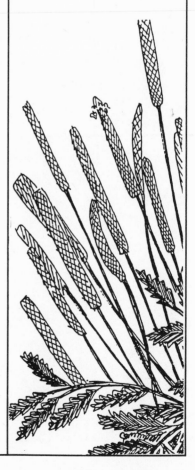

Cheese Wafers with Pecans

2 cups sharp cheddar cheese, grated

1 stick butter, softened

1½ cups unbleached flour

dash Tabasco

½ teaspoon salt

dash cayenne pepper

dash paprika

36 whole pecan halves

Mix the cheese with the butter, flour, Tabasco, salt, cayenne pepper, and paprika. Chill the dough. Roll out on a lightly floured board and cut with a biscuit cutter. Top each wafer with a whole pecan half and bake at 325° for 15–20 minutes.

Yields approximately 3 dozen

Miniature Bran Muffins

1½ cups all-bran cereal

2 cups 40% bran flakes cereal

1 cup boiling water

½ cup oil

1½ cups sugar

2 eggs, beaten

2 cups buttermilk

2½ cups unbleached flour

1 teaspoon salt

2½ teaspoons baking soda

1 cup pecans, chopped

½ cup golden raisins

1. Preheat oven to 400°.
2. Put 1 cup of each cereal in a bowl and add boiling water. Let
   stand until cool. Mix in oil, the remaining cereals, sugar, eggs,
   and buttermilk. Sift flour, salt, and soda together and combine
   with mixture. Add the pecans and raisins.
3. Fill well-greased muffin tins about ⅔ full and bake for 20
   minutes at 400°.

Yields 3–4 dozen

Another time add ½ cup puréed banana to batter before baking, or ½ cup puréed cooked pumpkin.

Coffee Punch

This recipe from Maxine Fitch makes a delightful beverage for a summertime morning coffee.

2 quarts strong coffee

¾ cup sugar

½ pint heavy cream, whipped

1 cup chocolate syrup

1 quart vanilla ice cream

Make the coffee, add the sugar, and stir to dissolve. Cool. Freeze some of this mixture in a ring mold to use in the punch bowl.

Just before serving, mix the coffee with the whipped cream, the chocolate syrup, and the ice cream cut into chunks. Stir well and pour into a large punch bowl. Add the frozen coffee ring and garnish with fresh flowers.

Yields 30 cups

Summer Seafood Dinner

Lemon Balm Summer Cooler

* * *

Small Fry Crab Cakes with
Tarragon-Chive Mayonnaise

* * *

Red Snapper with Matchstick Vegetables

Lemon Rice with Almonds

Cornbread Muffins with Bacon

* * *

Grand Marnier Sherbet with Orange Mint Nougatine

Icebox Cookies

Serves 6–8 people

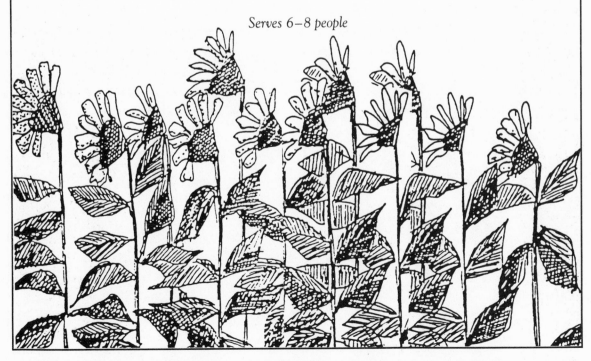

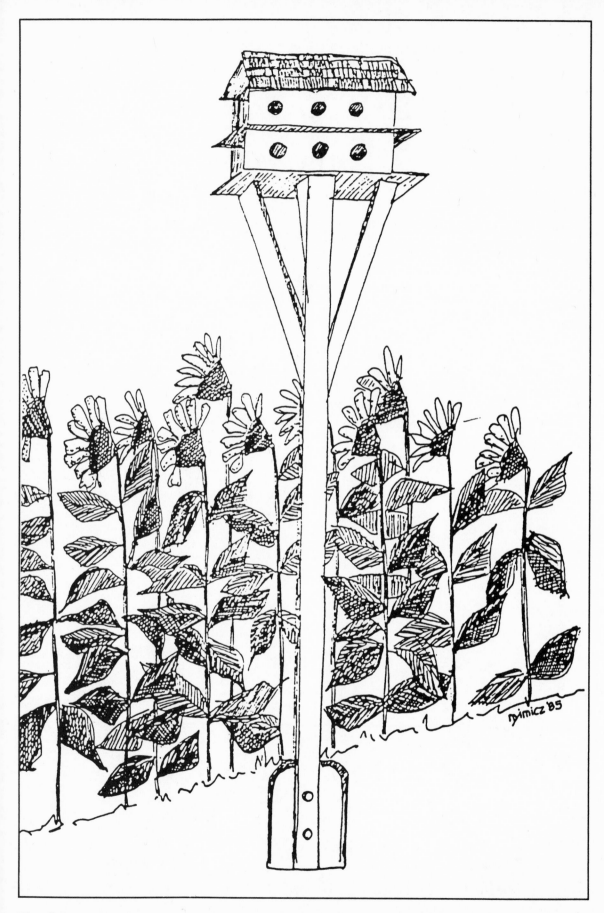

Lemon Balm Summer Cooler

½ quart boiling water

2 blackberry tea bags

¼ cup sugar

¼ cup lemon balm leaves

¼ cup lemon juice, freshly squeezed

3 ounces frozen lemonade

1 bottle (750 ml) white wine

optional: **extra lemon balm leaves for garnish**

1. Make the tea with boiling water, tea bags, sugar, and bruised lemon balm leaves, stirring often to dissolve the sugar. Steep for 5 minutes. Strain and cool.
2. Mix lemon juice, lemonade, and wine with the blackberry tea. Chill.
3. To serve, pour over ice in tall stemmed goblets and garnish with fresh lemon balm leaves.

6–8 portions

Summer Flower Arranging Tip
Cutting and Conditioning Flowers

Since flowers should be conditioned before using them in an arrangement, it is a good idea to cut them early in the morning or late in the afternoon. Flowers cut at midday have given up a lot of moisture and strength because of the heat. Let the flowers sit in water for several hours to produce stronger blossoms for use in an arrangement.

If possible, take a container of lukewarm water to the garden so that stems may be placed in it as soon as they are cut. Lukewarm water is the most quickly absorbed.

Cut flowers with a knife (scissors may crush the stems and interfere with water absorption), and on a slant for better intake of water. Cut garden flowers just above a leaf node so that new growth can come from that point. Cut roses just before a stem that has five leaves on it, since flowers are produced on the stems that grow from the five-leaf juncture.

When to cut is a matter of preference. Roses, for example, may fail to open if the bud is too tight when cut; if cut just before the bud unfurls, the flower will last longer. Remove all foliage that will be below the waterline to prevent decaying. Thorns from roses can be snapped off as well as cut.

Wildflowers, woody stems, and many weeds such as Joe-Pye weed, ironweed, and pokeberry respond to very hot water when being condi-

(Continued on p. 79)

Small Fry Crab Cakes with Tarragon-Chive Mayonnaise

8 ounces lump crabmeat

¼ cup celery, finely chopped

¼ cup green or red pepper, finely chopped

4 scallions, minced

1 teaspoon lemon juice

¼ teaspoon salt, freshly ground white pepper

1½ tablespoons mayonnaise

1½ tablespoons butter, melted

1¼ cups bread crumbs

2 tablespoons egg, beaten

1 teaspoon dijon mustard

½ teaspoon Worcestershire sauce

1 tablespoon chives, chopped

1 tablespoon butter

1 recipe Tarragon-Chive Mayonnaise

1. Carefully pick over the crabmeat to remove any pieces of cartilage. Squeeze crabmeat in small batches to remove excess water.
2. Add the remaining ingredients except for the last two, mix, and shape into 1½″ × 2½″ × ½″ thick cakes.
3. Sauté in butter until lightly browned. Serve with tarragon-chive mayonnaise.

12 portions

Tarragon-Chive Mayonnaise

1 whole egg

½ teaspoon dijon mustard

¼ teaspoon salt

1 tablespoon fresh chives, minced

1 tablespoon fresh tarragon, minced

½ lemon rind, grated

½ small clove garlic, minced

2 tablespoons lemon juice

½ cup vegetable oil

½ cup olive oil

1. Place the egg in a blender and process for about 2 minutes until the mixture is thick and sticky.
2. Add mustard, salt, herbs, lemon rind, garlic, and lemon juice and blend.
3. With the machine still running, use a baster to add the oil drop by drop until over half the oil has been added and the mixture thickens. Add the rest of the oil in a steady stream.

Yields approximately 1 cup

If the mayonnaise refuses to thicken or has curdled, blend together 1 teaspoon prepared mustard and 1 tablespoon of the mayonnaise in a clean bowl. Beat for a few seconds until the sauce has thickened or smoothed. Add the rest of the turned sauce by the teaspoon, beating after each addition.

Flower Arranging Tip
(continued)

tioned. Wrap the flowerheads loosely in newspaper so that steam will not damage them. Dip 2" of the stems in boiling water for 30 seconds, then plunge them in room-temperature water for several hours.

Flowers such as poppies or dahlias have hollow stems that must be seared by holding the stem over an open flame. This cuts the flow of the sap and prevents wilting.

Butterfly weed, hollyhocks, and dandelions exude a milky or sticky substance when cut. The ends of the stems must be sealed by holding them in boiling water for a few minutes. Finish conditioning in room-temperature water.

Branches should be cut with slits in the stem to improve water absorption. The old method of hammering the ends of the stems produces decay.

Some foliage responds well to being completely submerged. Elaeagnus, acuba, boxwood, some vines, and ivy may be soaked overnight in a bathtub before being used in arrangements.

Green Beans and Okra
in an Herbed Vinaigrette *

Served as a first course in the summertime at Fearrington House, green beans and okra would make a good alternative to crabcakes as a first course for this menu.

> 1 pound tiny green beans
>
> ½ pound okra
>
> 2 fresh tomatoes
>
> 2 tablespoons fresh tarragon, minced
>
> 2 tablespoons fresh parsley, minced
>
> 1 tablespoon chives, minced
>
> 1 recipe Vinaigrette (p. 33)

1. Cook beans in boiling salted water for 2 minutes. Drain in a colander and refresh with cold water; set aside.
2. Cook okra in boiling salted water for 2 minutes. Drain, refresh, and set aside.
3. Plunge the tomatoes into boiling water for 30–60 seconds until the skin bursts. Remove with a slotted spoon to a container of cold water. When the tomatoes are cool enough to handle, peel the skins. Find the pockets of seeds and remove them. Drain and chop into small pieces.
4. To assemble, arrange the beans on a serving plate in a neat bundle. Cut the okra crosswise in rounds and sprinkle across the beans. Arrange the tomatoes in a band across the beans; sprinkle with herbs and 2 tablespoons vinaigrette.

6–8 portions

* Extra Recipe

Red Snapper with Matchstick Vegetables

This is simply a perfect way to put almost a whole meal in a paper bag and is a foolproof way to cook fish. Cut the packets away with scissors just before serving. The aroma, which is released all at once, is heavenly.

2 tablespoons butter

1½ pounds fresh red snapper

¼ teaspoon salt, freshly ground white pepper

2 shallots, finely minced

12 sprigs lemon thyme

2 cups mixed vegetables (carrots, yellow squash, zucchini, red bell pepper), cut into matchstick pieces

3 ounces snow peas, cut into diagonal pieces

3 ounces white wine

1 lemon, sliced into 6 portions

6 pieces parchment paper, 9″ × 12″

6 pieces string, 6″ long

1. Preheat oven to 400°.
2. Cut 1 tablespoon butter into thin shavings and divide it among the pieces of parchment.
3. Cut the fish into six 4-ounce servings and place on top of the butter, skin side down. Season with salt and pepper.
4. Sprinkle minced shallots and lemon thyme over the fish. Surround the fish with the matchstick vegetables and snow peas. Pour 1 tablespoon wine over each fish and top with a lemon slice.
5. Completely enclose the fish in the parchment paper by loosely rolling the paper. Fold the ends and use the strings to tie them together like a handle. Make sure the paper has not torn.
6. Bake at 400° for 15–20 minutes. Transfer from the baking dish to a warmed platter. Cut the packets open just before serving.

6 portions

Cooking Shrimp

From 2 to 2½ pounds of green (uncooked, unshelled) shrimp will yield about 2 cups of cleaned, cooked shrimp.

2 pounds shrimp

2 quarts water

2 tablespoons cider vinegar

2 ribs celery

1 tablespoon pickling spice, tied in a cheesecloth square

1 bay leaf

Bring the water to a boil with the vinegar, celery, and spices.

Add the shrimp and watch carefully. As the water begins to simmer and the shrimp turn pink (about 3 minutes), they are fully cooked. Never let the water return to a full boil or the shrimp will be tough.

Refresh under cold water, drain and shell. Chill until serving time.

6 portions

From the shade garden

Garlic Mayonnaise *

2 egg yolks

1½ teaspoons dijon mustard

4 cloves garlic, minced

1 tablespoon tarragon vinegar

1 teaspoon salt, freshly ground white pepper

dash of Tabasco

1–1½ cups olive oil

1. Put the yolks in the bottom of a blender. Add the mustard, garlic, vinegar, salt, pepper, and Tabasco.
2. Blend at high speed for 30 seconds and then begin adding the oil drop by drop with a baster. After about ½ of the oil has been added in this manner, the sauce will begin to thicken and the rest of the oil may then be added in a slow, steady stream.

Yields approximately 1¾ cups

* Extra Recipe

Lemon Rice with Almonds

⅓ cup onion, minced

1 tablespoon butter

1 cup rice

1¾ cups chicken broth

¼ cup lemon juice

1 lemon rind, grated

¼ cup slivered almonds, lightly toasted

1. Sauté the onion in butter over moderate heat for about 5 minutes until it is translucent but not browned.
2. Blend in the rice and stir until all the grains are coated.
3. Add chicken broth, lemon juice, and lemon rind. Bring to a boil, lower heat, and simmer covered for about 20 minutes until all the liquid is absorbed. Blend in almonds and serve.

6 portions

For a more pungent flavor, try the garlic mayonnaise with the crabcakes on another occasion. It also makes a perfect dipping sauce for boiled shrimp or fish.

Summer Flower Arrangement
The Shade Garden

Caladium
Hosta
Fern
Galax
Aspidistra
Pachysandra
Palm
Bamboo
Ivy
False grapevine
Lichen
Moss from the woods
Begonias
Violet leaves

To condition the material for this arrangement, let the components sit in room-temperature water for several hours before arranging them.

The dough board is lined with plastic. Several pieces of soaked oasis hold the plant material.

Cornbread Muffins with Bacon

2 eggs

2 cups buttermilk

4 tablespoons butter, melted

½ cup unbleached flour, sifted

½ teaspoon baking soda

1 teaspoon sugar

2 teaspoons baking powder

¾ teaspoon salt

1½ cups yellow cornmeal

2 tablespoons chives, minced

2 ounces bacon, fried, drained, and chopped

1. Preheat oven to 450°.
2. Beat eggs and add buttermilk and butter to them. Sift flour, soda, sugar, baking powder, and salt together and add along with the rest of the ingredients. Whisk until smooth but do not overmix.
3. Pour into 2" well-greased muffin cups, filling almost to the top, and bake at 450° for 20–25 minutes.

Yields 2 dozen muffins

Grand Marnier Sherbet with Orange Mint Nougatine

Sherbet

1 cup water

⅔ cup sugar

1 orange rind, minced

2 cups orange juice

¼ cup lemon juice

½ cup heavy cream

2 tablespoons Grand Marnier

Orange Mint Nougatine

½ cup sugar

1 cup water

¼ cup orange mint
leaves, minced

Garnish

1 orange rind, cut into matchstick pieces

1. Bring 1 cup water and ⅔ cup sugar to a boil and cook until sugar is dissolved. Cool. Add the minced orange rind, orange juice, and lemon juice. Blend in the heavy cream and Grand Marnier.
2. Dissolve the remaining sugar and water together, and poach the matchstick pieces of orange rind in the resulting syrup for 3 minutes. Remove with a slotted spoon and set on a rack to drain. Add the minced orange mint leaves to the poaching syrup. Cook slowly until the sugar begins to caramelize and turn a light brown color. Remove from the heat and pour onto a lightly greased pan or marble slab. When it has hardened, break it into hunks and grind in a mortar until pieces are the size of peas.
3. Mix the caramelized mint with the orange mixture and freeze in an ice cream machine.
4. To serve, spoon the sherbet into 6 stemmed balloon wine goblets and top with the poached peel. Serve with 2 icebox cookies and extra orange mint as a garnish, if desired.

Yields approximately 1 quart

Caramelizing the Syrup

One needs to be observant to detect the exact moment of caramelizing. You may turn your back for a minute, only to find a blackened mass that takes soaking to remove from the pan.

As the syrup bubbles slowly in the pan, it begins to reduce and thicken. Some people think it gives off an extra puff of smoke just as the process is taking place. At any rate, the browning begins on one side of the pan and spreads across. Immediately lift the pan from the heat and swirl the mass, letting the heat stored in the pan continue the process. Pour the hot caramelized syrup on a lightly greased surface to harden.

For a different kind of ice-box cookie, change the flavor by mixing in 2 tablespoons grated orange rind and sub-stituting almonds for the pecans.

Icebox Cookies

When I was a child, my mother would mix the batter for these cookies, shape it into a log, and refrigerate the log. Later I would be allowed to slice and bake what was needed for a given occasion. We froze the rest for another time.

½ cup sugar

½ cup brown sugar

¾ cup butter, softened

2 eggs

1½ teaspoons vanilla

2¾ cups unbleached flour

½ teaspoon baking soda

¼ teaspoon salt

½–¾ cup pecans, chopped

1. Preheat oven to 400°.
2. Cream the sugars with butter until light and fluffy. Add eggs and vanilla. Sift the flour, soda, and salt and add them with the pecans to the mixture, blending well.
3. Shape into a log 2½″ in diameter, wrap in wax paper, and chill overnight.
4. Cut in thin slices and place the slices on an ungreased baking sheet. Bake 6–8 minutes at 400°.

Yields 5–6 dozen cookies

August Ice Cream Party

Vanilla Ice Cream With Lucinda's
Chocolate Sauce

Blackberry Ice Cream With Candied Lemon Peel

Lemon Ice Cream With Strawberry Sauce

Butter Cookies

Almond Crisps

Serves 10–12 people

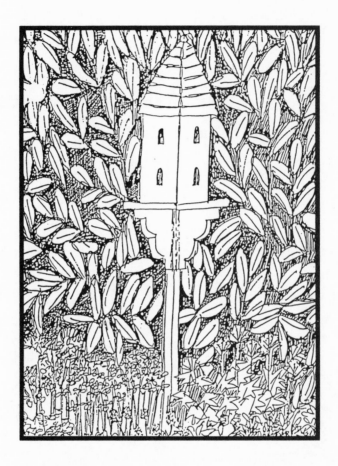

Vanilla Ice Cream
with Lucinda's Chocolate Sauce

4 cups milk

2 tablespoons unbleached flour

1½ cups sugar

½ teaspoon salt

4 eggs

1 cup heavy cream

1 teaspoon vanilla

extra milk if needed

1 recipe Lucinda's Chocolate Sauce

1. Scald milk in a saucepan over moderate heat.
2. Mix flour, sugar, and salt together in a bowl until the flour is completely mixed and there are no lumps; combine with 4 slightly beaten eggs.
3. Whisk while pouring about 1 cup of the hot milk into the egg-sugar mixture. Slowly pour all the contents of the bowl back into the saucepan. (Pouring a little hot liquid into the eggs helps keep them from cooking all at once.) Cook over medium heat for about 15–20 minutes, stirring constantly until the mixture thickens and heavily coats the back of a spoon. Cool. Add heavy cream and vanilla.
4. To freeze, pour the liquid mixture into the freezing compartment of a large 4-quart ice cream freezer and add milk (or milk mixed with heavy cream if a richer version is desired) until the freezer is ¾ full. Surround with ice and salt and freeze.
5. To serve, spoon into individual bowls and ladle warm chocolate sauce over the top.

Yields approximately 4 quarts

Other varieties of ice cream that can be made with this recipe include peach, banana, chocolate, and peppermint.

Peach Ice Cream

Omit the vanilla and add 3 cups of puréed peaches plus ¼ teaspoon almond extract to the custard base. Fill with milk as directed.

Banana Ice Cream

Add 3 puréed bananas to the custard base. Fill as directed.

Chocolate Ice Cream

Melt two 1-ounce squares of semisweet chocolate. Cool and add to egg-sugar mixture before it is added to the hot liquid. Proceed as directed.

Peppermint Ice Cream

Place 6 ounces peppermint candy in a plastic bag and crush with a hammer. Omit the vanilla from the master recipe, cut the sugar in the base to 1 cup, and add 1–2 drops oil of peppermint (available at the pharmacy).

The sauce hardens when spooned over ice cream. It becomes very thick when cooled. It may also be made in advance and refrigerated. To warm, set storage container in a pan of water over very low heat, stirring occasionally.

Another time make Lucinda's Chocolate Sauce without the vanilla and divide it in half. Add different liqueurs to the two halves as suggested below, and offer guests a choice of two sauces for their vanilla ice cream.

Chocolate Coffee Sauce

Blend 2 teaspoons instant coffee crystals into the hot sauce and stir until melted. Add 2 tablespoons Kahlua.

Grand Marnier Chocolate Sauce

Blend in 1 tablespoon finely grated orange rind and 2 tablespoons Grand Marnier (or to taste). Or try omitting the grated orange rind from the sauce and serving it instead with thinly sliced pieces of candied orange peel.

Lucinda's Chocolate Sauce

2 tablespoons butter

½ cup heavy cream

4 tablespoons corn syrup

1 cup sugar

4 ounces unsweetened chocolate

½ cup boiling water

2 teaspoons vanilla

1. Melt the butter over low heat in a medium saucepan.
2. Blend in the heavy cream, corn syrup, sugar, and chocolate and stir over low heat until the sugar is almost dissolved.
3. Bring the mixture to a simmer, add the boiling water, and briefly blend the two mixtures. Cook over medium heat for 5 minutes without stirring.
4. Remove from the heat and let cool slightly. Add vanilla.

Yields approximately 1 ¼ cups

Blackberry Ice Cream
with Candied Lemon Peel

2 lemon rinds

½ cup sugar

1 cup water

2 pints blackberries

1 cup sugar

2–3 teaspoons cassis

1½ lemons, juiced

1½ cups heavy cream

1. Remove the rind from the lemons with a vegetable peeler in vertical strips, peeling from tip to tip. Cut into thin matchstick pieces.
2. Dissolve the sugar in the water and bring to a boil. Cook the lemon peel strips for 15-18 minutes until the syrup begins to caramelize (see p. 85 for caramelizing the syrup). Remove with a slotted spoon, and let cool on a rack.
3. Purée the blackberries in a food processor and push the pulp through a strainer to remove the seeds. Combine with sugar, cassis, lemon juice, and heavy cream. Chop the lemon rind and add to the base.
4. Freeze for about 20 minutes in an electric ice cream machine.

Yields ¾ quart

(see p. 85 for caramelizing the syrup)

From the Wildflower Field

An attractive summer arrangement that is both fresh and crisp can be made from the following wildflowers and weeds:

Pokeberry
Queen Anne's Lace
Lespadeza
Pink coneflower
White coneflower
Black-eyed Susan
Goldenrod
Butterfly weed
Native sunflower

The pokeberry, coneflowers, black-eyed Susans, butterfly weed, and native sunflowers need to be immersed in almost boiling water for 30–60 seconds and then left to condition for several hours in room-temperature water.

From the wildflower field

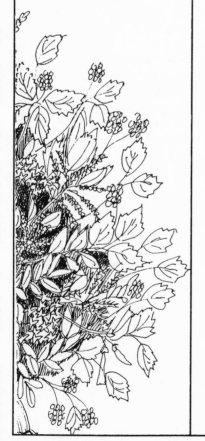

This ice cream reaches perfection with the addition of caramelized lemon peel. Add just before freezing. See blackberry ice cream recipe (p. 91) for instructions.

Lemon Ice Cream
with Strawberry Sauce

1 lemon rind, grated

⅔ cup sugar

1½ cups milk

2 cups heavy cream, heated

5 egg yolks

⅔ cup freshly squeezed lemon
   juice (3–4 lemons)

1 recipe Strawberry Sauce

1. Blend the grated lemon rind with the sugar.
2. Put the lemon, sugar, milk, and 1½ cups heavy cream in a saucepan. Bring to a boil, stirring occasionally to dissolve the sugar.
3. Whisk the egg yolks in a bowl and slowly pour about half the hot cream into the bowl, stirring constantly. Pour the contents of the bowl back into the saucepan and continue to cook over low heat, stirring constantly for 10–15 minutes until the mixture heavily coats the back of a spoon and becomes thickened. Do not let the mixture boil. Cool.
4. When the mixture is cool, add the lemon juice and the rest of the heavy cream. Freeze.
5. To serve, spoon ice cream into individual bowls and ladle sauce over the top.

Yields 1 quart ice cream

Strawberry Sauce

1 quart fresh strawberries

1 cup superfine sugar

2 tablespoons kirsch

Wash, drain, and decap the berries.

Purée in a food processor and push through a strainer to remove the seeds.

Put the purée in a food processor, add the sugar, and process for about 2 minutes to dissolve the sugar.

Blend in the kirsch.

Yields approximately 2 cups

Basic Butter Cookies

8 ounces butter, softened

¾ cup sugar

1 teaspoon vanilla

2 egg yolks

2¼ cups flour, sifted

½ teaspoon salt

1. Preheat oven to 350°.
2. Cream butter and sugar. Add vanilla and egg yolks and mix well, gradually adding flour and salt.
3. If the cookies are to be piped with a cookie gun or pastry bag, use dough immediately. If the dough is to be rolled and cut into shapes, chill for 2 hours before rolling.
4. Bake cookies at 350° on parchment paper about 15–20 minutes until they are lightly browned.

Yields approximately 5 dozen cookies

Karen Barker

As a variation you can add 1 tablespoon finely grated lemon or orange rind or 1½ tablespoons poppy seeds.

Gilding the Lily— Toppings for Ice Cream

A little imagination can turn a fairly simple dessert into a very special one. Homemade vanilla ice cream topped with fresh peach slices and melba sauce will far outclass any version of peach melba simply because fresh fruit is used.

Blueberries, blackberries, or raspberries also go well with homemade ice cream. Sliced strawberries and vanilla ice cream served on top of brownies make a wonderful combination; add raspberry sauce and it becomes memorable.

Other good combinations are blueberry sauce (p. 46) with lemon ice cream and vanilla ice cream with fresh blackberries and raspberry sauce (p. 169). A fruit sorbet topped with a fruit sauce says summertime in an emphatic way.

For a special after-dinner treat, a little brandy or liqueur over ice cream (such as Kahlua over chocolate ice cream) may be all that's needed.

Chocolate sauce, caramel sauce, pecan praline, pistachios, or chocolate shavings add a special touch. Candied violets or rose petals can add delightful color. Garnish a colorful sorbet with just the right flower and people will long remember the dessert.

Almond Praline

½ cup sugar

1 cup water

1 cup slivered almonds

1. Bring the sugar and water to a boil and simmer until the sugar dissolves. Add almonds and cook until the syrup thickens and begins to turn golden brown.
2. Pour into an oiled pan and cool until hard.
3. Turn out of the pan and break into chunks. Cover the chunks with wax paper and crush with a rolling pin or grind them into small pieces in a mortar.
4. Store in a glass jar with a tight-fitting lid.

Yields approximately 4 ounces

Almond Crisps

2 cups sugar

1½ sticks butter

½ teaspoon lemon rind, grated

1 egg

2 teaspoons vanilla

pinch of salt

2 cups flour

1 cup thinly sliced almonds

1. Preheat oven to 350°.
2. Cream sugar and butter together until the mixture is light and fluffy. Add the lemon rind, egg, and vanilla and blend well.
3. Combine the salt and flour and mix with the butter-sugar mixture. Stir in the almonds and spread the mixture into a 12″ × 9″ pan.
4. Bake at 350° for about 30 minutes. Remove from the oven and cut immediately into 3″ × 1″ bars. Allow to cool slightly and finish crisping on a cake rack.

Yields 36 bars

Summer Evening with Music

Fearrington House Cooler

*   *   *

Chilled Tomato Soup with Basil Sorbet

*   *   *

Shrimp and Scallops in Scallop Pastry Shells

Snow Peas and Sugar Snaps in Lemon Thyme Butter

Squash Gratin with White Cheddar Cheese

*   *   *

Shortbread with Lemon Curd and Blackberry Sauce

Serves 6 people

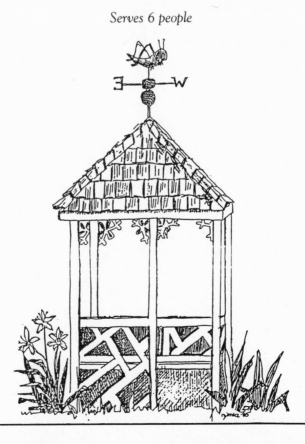

Chilled Tomato Soup
with Basil Sorbet

2 tablespoons butter

1 onion, chopped

1 leek, chopped

2 carrots, chopped

3–3½ pounds fresh tomatoes, peeled,
    seeded, and chopped

1 orange rind, grated

1–2 drops Tabasco

½ teaspoon salt, freshly ground pepper

2 cups water

1 cup chicken stock

1 bouquet garni (basil, thyme,
    parsley, chives, summer savory, and dill)

1½ cups heavy cream

1 recipe Basil Sorbet

1. Melt the butter in a large saucepan and add the onion, leek, and carrots. Cook over medium heat about 8 minutes or until soft and translucent but not browned.
2. Add the chopped tomatoes, orange rind, Tabasco, salt, pepper, water, and chicken stock. Make a bouquet garni by tying the herbs in a square piece of cheesecloth. Cover and simmer 30–40 minutes over a low flame. Remove the bouquet garni and set the soup aside to cool.
3. Purée in a blender or food processor. Cool to room temperature and add the heavy cream. Chill.
4. To serve, ladle soup into individual bowls. Place a scoop of basil sorbet in the center of each. Garnish with fresh basil.

6 portions

Fearrington House Cooler

1 bottle (750 ml)
* white wine*

2 peaches

handful of assorted
* mints: orange,*
* spearmint*

1. Place the peaches in boiling water a few seconds so that the skin can be easily removed.

2. Remove the skin and place the whole fruit in a pitcher with the wine and mints. Let steep 4 hours before serving.

3. Pour over ice in stemmed goblets and garnish each with a sprig of mint or a peach slice.

6 portions

Summertime in the South means grilling outdoors, tomatoes, berry picking, homemade ice creams, and the freshest vegetables possible. It is time to make herbed vinegars and oils, freeze compound butters, and make basil sauce to be used in winter.

Basil Sorbet

½ cup sugar

1½ cups water

juice of 2 lemons

2 lemon rinds, grated

½ cup parsley, finely minced

1½ cups basil, finely minced

fresh basil leaves for garnish

1. Make a syrup by dissolving the sugar in the water and bringing it to a boil. Cool.
2. Combine remaining ingredients with the syrup. Freeze.

Yields approximately 2 cups

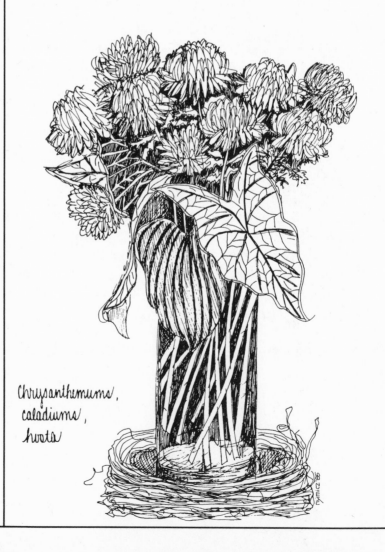

Chrysanthemums, caladiums, hosta

Shrimp and Scallops
in Scallop Pastry Shells

Prepare pastry shells and shrimp a day ahead. The actual cooking takes only minutes, since the seafood needs to be cooked quickly.

3 tablespoons butter

1 tablespoon olive oil

2 large shallots, minced

2 large cloves of garlic, minced

⅓ cup green bell pepper, minced

⅓ cup red bell pepper (if available), minced

3 ounces mushrooms, minced

1 medium-size carrot, minced

1 sprig fresh thyme

¾ cup dry white wine

¼ teaspoon salt, freshly ground pepper

1 pound scallops, cleaned and with beards removed

½ pound shrimp, cleaned and cooked

6-8 cherry tomatoes, halved and deseeded

1 tablespoon mixed herbs (tarragon, parsley, chervil, chives), minced

1 recipe Scallop Pastry Shells

1. Melt the butter in a skillet, add olive oil, and sauté the shallots and garlic over medium heat for 2 minutes.
2. Add the peppers, mushrooms, carrots, and thyme. Cook about 10 minutes or until crispy tender.
3. Incorporate the wine and raise the heat to reduce the liquid slightly. Blend in the salt and pepper.
4. Add the scallops and cook over low heat for 1–2 minutes. Mix in the shrimp and cherry tomatoes and heat through.
5. At the last minute divide the mixture among the scallop pastry shells and serve immediately. Garnish with minced herbs.

6 portions

Partially Baked Pie Shells

To partially bake a pie shell, preheat the oven to 425°. Dock the bottom of the shell with a fork, cover with wax paper or parchment, and fill with pie weights, being careful to distribute the weights against the walls to help keep the crust from shrinking. Bake for 12–15 minutes or until golden.

Scallop Pastry Shells

Natural scallop shells (which are used as molds in this recipe) are available at most kitchen supply stores, since they are commonly used for coquilles St. Jacques.

12 scallop shells   **1 recipe Never-Fail Pastry**

1. Preheat oven to 425°.
2. Roll pastry to ⅛″ thickness. Cut into 6 circles roughly 2″ larger in diameter than the scallop shells. Ease the circle into the shell, shaping it to the exact dimensions of the shell. Trim off excess pastry.
3. Prick the shell and weight it (to keep from shrinking) by placing an empty scallop shell on top.
4. Bake at 425° for about 10 minutes. Remove the top shell and continue baking until the pastry is golden brown. Carefully remove the pastry from the shell and cool on a rack.

Yields 6 shells

Never-Fail Pastry

This dough may be kept in the refrigerator for 3 days or frozen. No matter how much it is handled, it will always be flaky and tender. When it is rolled, it behaves exactly as desired.

2 cups unbleached flour   **1 egg**

1½ teaspoons sugar   **¼ cup water**

1 teaspoon salt   **1½ teaspoons vinegar**

6 ounces vegetable shortening

1. Mix the flour, sugar, and salt together with a pastry blender. Cut the shortening into the mixture until the pieces resemble coarse meal.
2. In a separate bowl beat the egg with the water and vinegar.
3. Combine the two mixtures by tossing with two forks until all the ingredients are moistened and may be gathered into a ball. Chill before rolling.

Yields two 9″ pie crusts

Snow Peas and Sugar Snaps in Lemon Thyme Butter

2 tablespoons butter, softened

½ teaspoon lemon juice

½ teaspoon parsley, finely minced

1½ teaspoons lemon thyme, finely minced

6 ounces snow peas

12 ounces sugar snap peas

1. Mix the butter with the lemon juice, parsley, and lemon thyme, and set aside.
2. String both the snow peas and the sugar snaps on both ends. Cook the snow peas in boiling water for about 1 minute, drain in a colander, and refresh under cold water briefly to stop the cooking process. Cook the sugar snaps for about 2 minutes, drain, and refresh briefly under cold water.
3. Mix the snow peas and the sugar snaps together while still warm, and toss with the herbed butter. Serve immediately.

6 portions

The Gray Garden

This arrangement focuses on texture and shape. All the plant material is gray. There is only one blossom (mullein) in the entire arrangement.

Lamb's ear
Mullein
Southern wormwood
Dusty miller
Gray santolina
Spanish moss
Lichen

To condition the material for this arrangement, the lamb's ear, wormwood, dusty miller, and santolina need to be put in room-temperature water as soon as they are cut and left to sit for several hours. The mullein should have 2" of its stem held in almost boiling water for about 1 minute and then be put in room-temperature water for several hours.

Spanish moss and plastic line the basket. Soaked oasis holds the flowers.

From the gray garden

Edible Flowers

Borage *blossoms and leaves taste a little like cucumbers. Young leaves may be used in salads or as a substitute for spinach. The star-shaped blue flowers are used in salads or soups, as decorations, or as flavoring agents for beverages.*

Calendula *flowers are used fresh or dried in salads and soups, and are sometimes used to color foods as a substitute for saffron.*

Camomile *flowers have a daisy-like appearance and an apple fragrance and flavor. They are popularly used as a tea that is said to have a soothing sedative effect.*

Chive *flowers and spears are added to salads and butters to lend light onion flavor. Chive flowerheads are used to make an herbed vinegar that is noteworthy for its pretty pink color.*

Dandelion *flowers and leaves, which appear in the early spring, have a very high vitamin content. They are used in salads.*

Marigolds *are high in phosphorus and vitamin C. They are used in cooking for their color and distinctive flavor in salads, soups, and rice.*

Nasturtiums *also are very high in vitamin C. The flowers and leaves are used in salads and as an all-purpose garnish. Both have a spicy, pungent flavor.*

(Continued on p. 103)

Squash Gratin with White Cheddar Cheese

1 medium-size onion, thinly sliced

2 pounds yellow squash, thinly sliced

1 teaspoon salt, freshly ground pepper

2 eggs

2 tablespoons sugar

½ cup milk

½ pound Vermont or New York white cheddar cheese, grated

1–2 tablespoons butter

1. Preheat oven to 350°.
2. Cook the onions and squash in a small amount of boiling water for 10–15 minutes or until fork-tender. Drain well. Arrange in a 2-quart baking dish. Add salt and pepper.
3. Mix eggs, sugar, milk, and cheese and pour over squash mixture. Dot with *thin* slices of butter.
4. Bake at 350° for 45 minutes. Cut into squares and then into diamonds to make a prettier shape on the plate.

6–8 portions

Shortbread with Lemon Curd and Blackberry Sauce

Each component of this special dessert is simple to prepare. The result is something available only during the summertime.

2 sticks butter, softened	¼ teaspoon almond extract
⅔ cup confectioners' sugar	1 recipe Lemon Curd
2 cups unbleached flour	1 recipe Blackberry Sauce
pinch of salt	24 fresh blackberries

1. Preheat oven to 325°.
2. Cream butter and sugar together until light and fluffy. Sift flour and salt together and add with almond extract to the butter-sugar mixture. Mix well.
3. Pat the dough into a 12¾″ × 9″ pan that has been lined with parchment paper. Bake at 325° for about 35–40 minutes or until the center feels firm when gently pressed. The shortbread should not brown.
4. Remove from the oven. Cut into 8 squares, and then cut each square into 2 triangles while still warm. Cool on a rack.
5. To serve, ladle ¼ cup blackberry sauce into a dessert plate. Top with 2 shortbread triangles, 2 tablespoons lemon curd, and 3 fresh blackberries. Garnish with a white or yellow marigold.

8 portions

Edible Flowers (continued)

Violet *blossoms can be candied for use as cake decorations. Used fresh, the white and blue flowers provide a garnish for beverages, salads, and desserts.*

Flowers of culinary herbs such as marjoram, oregano, summer savory, basil, thyme, and rosemary are used in salads, rice, pastas, and soups and as garnishes for many other dishes.

Blackberry Sauce

Use the blueberry sauce recipe on p. 46, substituting blackberries for the blueberries. Push the fresh blackberries through a strainer to remove the seeds.

The sauce will keep indefinitely in the refrigerator and may also be frozen.

Lemon Curd

5 egg yolks

¾ cup sugar

juice and grated rind of 2 large lemons

½ stick unsalted butter

1. Combine the egg yolks and sugar in a saucepan. Over low heat, gradually add the lemon juice, stirring constantly for 12–15 minutes until the mixture coats the back of a spoon and is thickened. (Do not let the mixture boil.)
2. Remove from the heat and continue stirring until slightly cool.
3. Cut the butter into small pieces and blend into the lemon mixture with the grated lemon rind. Cool and refrigerate.

Yields 1–1 ¼ cups

Garden Harvest Dinner

Cold Sliced Pork Tenderloin

Cold Sliced Roast Beef

Cold Sliced Baked Ham

Baked Stuffed Squash

Tina's Potato Salad with Green Beans
and Bacon

Fried Green Tomatoes

Summer Black-eyed Pea Salad

Southern Biscuit Muffins

*　　*　　*

Peach Cobbler with Cinnamon-Nutmeg Ice Cream

Serves 6–8 people

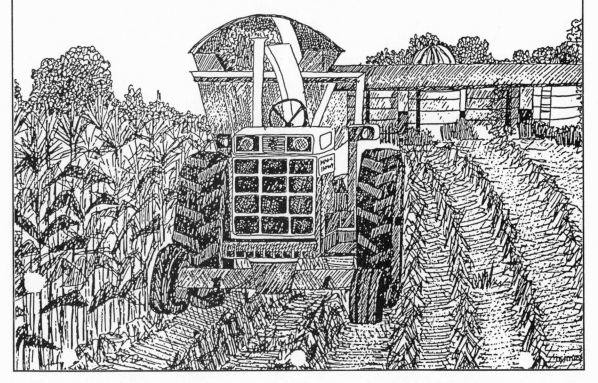

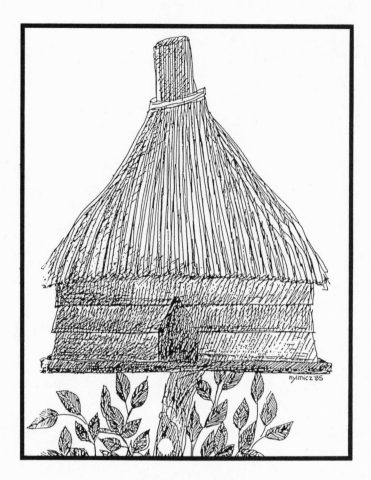

Thatched-roof birdhouse

Baked Stuffed Squash

At the wedding of one of my sisters, a cook appeared in the kitchen to help with the festivities; the outcome was the following recipe, which has been in our family for over 30 years. She herself had no recipe; she simply went into the kitchen to cook. Since we were smart enough to write down the proportions, we still enjoy the results today.

6 yellow crookneck squash

1 egg

1 tablespoon butter, melted

1 small onion, finely chopped

½ teaspoon salt, freshly ground white pepper

freshly grated nutmeg

⅛ teaspoon Worcestershire sauce

½ cup bread crumbs

2 tablespoons red or green
   bell pepper, minced

½ cup white cheddar cheese, grated

1. Preheat oven to 375°.
2. Bring water to a boil and cook the squash about 5 minutes until crispy tender. Drain.
3. When the squash are cool enough to handle, cut in half and scoop out the pulp, leaving ¼″ shells. Drain in a colander. Chop the pulp and combine with the rest of the ingredients.
4. Fill shells and bake for about 20 minutes at 375°.

6 portions

Chopped Herbs

Most of the time when a recipe calls for chopped herbs, it really means minced. The pieces should be chopped so finely that they are no longer identifiable. Parsley and chives are easy to mince, but big-leaf herbs (such as basil) need to be stacked on top of each other or gathered into a tight bundle before being minced.

Since fresh parsley is available most of the year at the grocery, mix dried herbs with it before chopping. The natural moisture in the fresh parsley helps reconstitute the dried herbs.

If a recipe calls for fresh herbs and you have only dried ones on hand, reduce the amount called for by 1/3.

Tina's Potato Salad
with Green Beans and Bacon

8 ounces bacon

2 pounds small red potatoes

¾ pound green beans

3 tablespoons basil-garlic vinegar (or red wine vinegar)

½ teaspoon salt

1 garlic clove, minced

1 teaspoon dijon mustard

½ teaspoon grainy mustard

½ cup olive oil

freshly ground pepper

¼ cup mixed herbs (parsley, summer savory, chives), finely minced

½ cup scallions, minced

¼–½ cup red bell pepper, minced

¼ cup fresh basil, finely minced

1. Fry bacon until crisp, drain on absorbent towels, and set aside.
2. Slice the potatoes ⅛″ thick and cook in boiling water over medium heat for 8–10 minutes. Drain.
3. Wash and string the beans. Cook in boiling water for 3–4 minutes until crispy tender. Refresh under cold water and drain.
4. To make the dressing, mix together the vinegar, salt, garlic, and the two types of mustard. Slowly whisk in the olive oil tablespoon by tablespoon. Add freshly ground pepper and the mixed herbs.
5. Combine the potatoes, green beans, scallions, and red peppers. Pour dressing over and let sit 2–3 hours.
6. Just before serving, chop the bacon and sprinkle it as well as the fresh basil on top.

6–8 portions

Fried Green Tomatoes

The amount of salt for this recipe seems exorbitant, but is necessary since the green tomatoes do not have much flavor. This is a good way to use green tomatoes that are on the vines late in the summer but will not ripen before the first frost.

6 medium-size fresh green
   tomatoes, cut into ¼″ slices

1½ cups buttermilk

1 cup cornmeal

½ cup unbleached flour

1 tablespoon salt,
   freshly ground pepper

1½ teaspoons cayenne pepper

2 teaspoons dried thyme

¼ cup peanut oil

¼ cup vegetable oil

1. Soak the tomato slices in buttermilk while mixing the cornmeal, flour, and spices together.
2. Dredge the tomato slices in the cornmeal mixture while the oils are heating in a large skillet. Sauté over medium heat for about 2 minutes per side or until golden. Drain on absorbent towels and serve immediately.

6 portions

Walter Royal

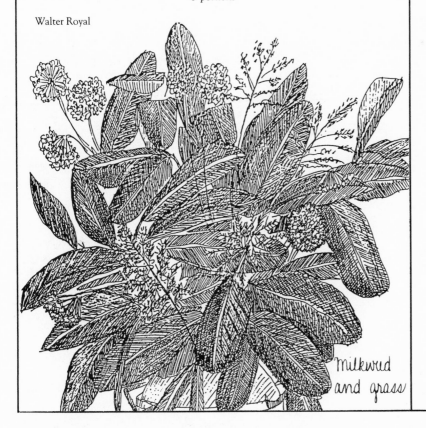

milkweed and grass

Milkweed is aptly named: as soon as it is cut, it begins to exude a milky substance. For proper conditioning, put 2″–3″ of the stems in simmering water and hold them there for about 1 minute. Hold the stems at an angle so that the steam will not affect the flowerheads. Watch the air bubbles as they come from the cut ends, and hold the stems in the pot until the bubbles cease.

If the stems are not seared or boiled, the milky substance will eventually make the cut stem unable to absorb water. In effect, the milky substance needs to be sealed in the plant cells.

Summer Black-eyed
Pea Salad

The vegetables used in this cold summer salad are well known to any Southerner; we have simply treated them in a different manner. The salad is colorful and delicious.

1½ cups dried black-eyed peas, soaked overnight

2 tablespoons olive oil

1 tablespoon dried herbes de Provence (available at specialty foods stores)

½ teaspoon salt, freshly ground pepper

4 ears fresh corn

1½ cups fresh lima beans

4 scallions, chopped

½ red bell pepper, minced

3 tablespoons fresh herbs (chives, summer savory, oregano), minced

1 recipe Vinaigrette (p. 33)

1. Soak the peas overnight with water to cover.
2. The next day drain and rinse, discarding any skins that floated to the top. Place 2½–3 cups of water in a 2½-quart saucepan and bring the peas to a boil. Season with olive oil, herbes de Provence, salt, and pepper. Reduce the heat and cook the peas at a slow simmer for 35–40 minutes. Drain and set aside.
3. Clean and desilk the corn. Blanch in boiling water for 3 minutes. Drain. Cut off the kernels and add to the black-eyed peas.
4. Cook the lima beans for about 10 minutes in boiling water. Drain and add to the corn and peas.
5. Season the mixture with the scallions, bell pepper, herbs, salt, and pepper. Pour the vinaigrette over and mix well.

6–8 portions

Southern Biscuit Muffins

2½ cups flour

3 tablespoons sugar

1½ tablespoons baking powder

¼ teaspoon salt

5 ounces butter, softened

1 cup cold milk

1. Preheat oven to 350°. Grease the muffin tins.
2. Combine flour, sugar, baking powder, and salt in a mixing bowl and blend well.
3. Add butter and cut in thoroughly.
4. Stir in milk just to mix. Do not overwork.
5. Fill the tins ⅔ full with batter. Bake at 350° for about 30 minutes or until lightly browned.

Yields 10 muffins

Karen Barker

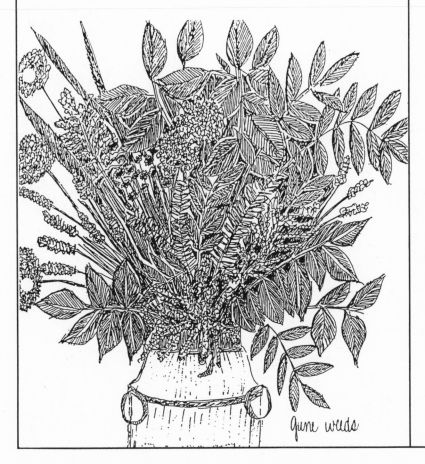

june weeds

Summer Flower Arrangement
June Weeds

As summer begins to arrive, some greens have been at their peak and are still holding after a month. Others, like dock, have matured and browned, and thus are no longer useful for our purposes.

By mid-June, the Queen Anne's Lace is beginning to close into urn-shaped, handsome seedheads. The blackberries are beginning to ripen and have a nice reddish color. Sumac has a whitish cast that seems to say "Summer," and the elderberries are changing from flowerheads to berry clusters.

Weeds that can be used in a June arrangement include:

Blackberries
Queen Anne's Lace
Grass
Sumac
Elderberry
Butterfly weed
Chokeberry
Trumpet vine
Field marguerite
Dandelion
White polygonum

To condition the material, hold the sumac, elderberry, butterfly weed, chokeberry, and trumpet vine stems in almost boiling water for 60 seconds until air bubbles stop coming from the cut end, and then place them in cold water for a few hours before arranging.

Peach Cobbler with Cinnamon-Nutmeg Ice Cream

Cobblers are old-fashioned desserts that were so named because of the method of dropping biscuit dough on top of the fruit. Our version is made with a buttery pie crust dough used only on top. The cobbler may be varied by adding fresh raspberries or blackberries or by serving it with heavy cream.

> ½ recipe All-Purpose Pastry (p. 53) with the following additions: 1½ ounces slivered almonds (finely chopped), ¼ teaspoon freshly grated nutmeg, and 1 tablespoon sugar
>
> 3–4 cups peaches
>
> juice of 1 lemon
>
> 3 tablespoons flour
>
> ⅔ cup sugar
>
> 1 lemon rind, grated
>
> freshly grated nutmeg
>
> 2 tablespoons unsalted butter
>
> 1 recipe Cinnamon-Nutmeg Ice Cream

1. Preheat oven to 400°.
2. Peel and slice the peaches and put in the bottom of an oval glass baking dish. Sprinkle with the lemon juice to keep the peaches from turning dark.
3. Mix the flour and sugar together and sprinkle along with the lemon rind over the peaches. Grate fresh nutmeg on top.
4. Fit the crust almost to the edges of the dish, dot with butter, and cut vents to allow steam to escape. Bake at 400° for 25–30 minutes until crust is browned.
5. Spoon the cobbler into bowls, top with a scoop of cinnamon-nutmeg ice cream, and serve immediately.

6–8 portions

Cinnamon-Nutmeg Ice Cream

3½ cups half-and-half cream

14 egg yolks

1½ cups sugar

½ teaspoon salt

3 cups cream

¼ cup apple brandy

1½ tablespoons vanilla

2 tablespoons ground cinnamon

½ teaspoon ground nutmeg

1. Heat half-and-half almost to a boil in a large heavy-bottomed stainless steel saucepan.
2. Meanwhile beat egg yolks, sugar, and salt in a mixer until thick and light. Lower speed and gradually add hot half-and-half into egg yolk mixture.
3. Transfer mixture back into saucepan and cook over low heat, stirring constantly until the custard coats the back of a spoon. Do not boil.
4. Remove from heat and add cream, apple brandy, vanilla, cinnamon, and nutmeg. Chill thoroughly. Before freezing, strain through a fine sieve, pressing spices through.
5. Freeze in an ice cream maker.

Yields approximately ½ gallon

Karen Barker

When the cinnamon is added to the liquid it floats to the top in lumps. The spices are pressed through a sieve to break them up and allow them to mix with the liquid ingredients.

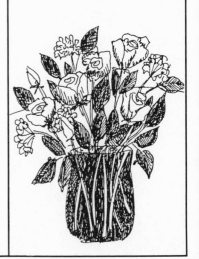

Labor Day Picnic

Carrots with Smooth Tomato Dressing

Onion, Leek, and Shallot Tart

Sweet Red Bell Peppers with Lentil Salad

Joaquin's Herbed Cheese

Picnic Basket Bread

*   *   *

Fresh Fruit with Grand Marnier Sauce

Serves 6–8 people

from the
herb garden

Carrots with Smooth Tomato Dressing

This is a very good "fix ahead" recipe. It will keep in the refrigerator 2 weeks in a covered container.

> 5 cups carrots, sliced diagonally in ⅜" slices
>
> 2 medium-size sweet onions, diced
>
> 1 small green pepper, diced
>
> 1 10½-ounce can tomato soup
>
> 1 cup sugar
>
> ½ cup salad oil
>
> ¾ cup vinegar
>
> 1 teaspoon Worcestershire sauce
>
> 1 teaspoon prepared mustard
>
> ½ teaspoon salt, freshly ground pepper

1. Cook carrots for about 8–10 minutes until crispy tender. Drain and cool. Mix with the onions and green peppers in a large bowl.
2. Combine remaining ingredients and pour over. Refrigerate for 12 hours to let flavors develop.

8–10 portions

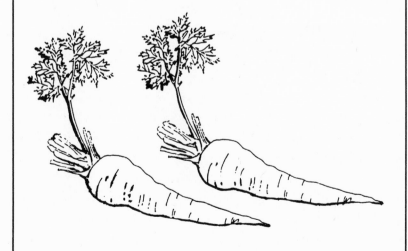

Summer Flower Arrangement
From the Herb Garden

Cut the herbs in mid-morning after the dew dries and put them immediately in warm water to condition for several hours.

Soak the oasis, put it in a large can, and fill the can to the top with water.

Herbs used:

Scented geraniums (two kinds)

Black fennel

Dill (with flowerheads)

Flowers of garlic chives

Basil

Summer savory

Southern wormwood

Orange mint

Spearmint

Peppermint with flowers

Strawberry foliage

Asparagus fern

Oregano flowers

Tansy

Leek flowerheads

Perennial sweetpea

Morning glory

Lamb's ear

Parsley with flowers (bolted)

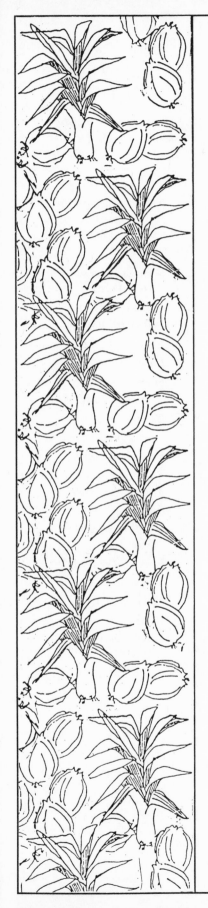

Onion, Leek, and Shallot Tart

1 partially baked Herbed Pie Crust shell, 15″ × 10½″ (recipe p. 53)

1 teaspoon dijon mustard

1 pound leeks, thinly sliced

3 ounces butter

2 tablespoons olive oil

1 pound onions, thinly sliced

4 ounces shallots, thinly sliced

2 cloves garlic, minced

½ teaspoon salt, freshly ground white pepper

4 ounces bacon, or 2 ounces country ham

4–6 scallions (green and white parts), minced

2 eggs

¾ cup heavy cream

freshly grated nutmeg to taste

½ teaspoon salt, freshly ground pepper

½ cup parmesan cheese, freshly grated

1 ounce Montrachet cheese

optional: 1 tablespoon fresh thyme, minced (or 1 teaspoon dried)

2 teaspoons butter

1. Preheat oven to 375°. Brush the partially baked shell with mustard and set aside.
2. Wash the leeks carefully under running water to remove any loose dirt; drain and trim.
3. Melt the butter in a heavy skillet and add the olive oil. Cook the leeks, onions, shallots, and garlic slowly over moderate heat for about 1 hour until the onions are almost caramelized and soft, but not browned. Add salt and pepper. Cool. Spread the mixture evenly over the partially baked tart shell.
4. Fry bacon until crisp. Drain, chop, and spread over the onions along with the scallions.
5. Lightly beat eggs and mix with heavy cream, fresh nutmeg, salt, and pepper. Pour over the onions and sprinkle with parmesan, Montrachet, and herbs. Dot with paper-thin slices of butter. Place whole tart on a round pizza pan, and bake at 375° for about 30–35 minutes or until golden.

8 portions

Sweet Red Bell Peppers
with Lentil Salad

This delightful salad gets better every day as the flavors sit and blend themselves together.

It is important that the lentils have not been sitting on the grocery shelf for a long time, since if they are stale they will quickly disintegrate while cooking. A health food store is perhaps the best place to buy these beans, since there is a faster turnover there.

The salad is prepared in two steps: marinating the cooked beans overnight and adding extra ingredients the next day.

For a variation, serve the lentil salad on a bed of fresh spinach and garnish with red bell pepper strips and/or cherry tomato halves.

12 ounces lentils	1 pint cherry tomatoes, halved and deseeded
3 teaspoons dried oregano	1 tablespoon fresh dill, finely minced
2 bunches scallions	
½ cup olive oil	1 tablespoon fresh chives, finely minced
3 ounces Balsamic vinegar	
3 ounces tarragon vinegar	6–8 ounces chèvre cheese
2 cloves garlic, finely minced	freshly ground pepper
1 carrot, finely chopped	6 red bell peppers

1. Wash and pick over the lentils, discarding the discolored ones. Boil them in salted water for about 8 minutes with 1 teaspoon dried oregano and 1 bunch whole scallions. It is important that the lentils be cooked only until they are crispy tender. Remove the scallions and discard. Rinse the lentils in cold water and drain completely.

2. Mix the olive oil with the vinegars, the garlic, and the remaining oregano. Pour over the lentils and let marinate overnight.

3. The next day add 1 bunch chopped scallions, the carrot, tomatoes, dill, chives, pepper, and half of the chèvre (crumbled). Taste for seasoning and add additional salt if necessary.

4. Wash the bell peppers, cut the tops off, and remove the membrane and seeds. Divide the lentil salad among the peppers and sprinkle the remaining crumbled chèvre on top.

6–8 portions

Joaquin Fowler

Mushroom Sausage Tart *

This tart might be used in combination with the leek and shallot tart for the picnic, depending on the appetites of the picnickers. The cheese pastry is an especially flavorful addition.

Use the All-Purpose Pastry recipe on p. 53 for the crust, mixing ½ cup grated sharp white cheddar cheese in with the flour just before the butter and shortening are added.

1 recipe partially baked cheddar cheese pastry shell, in a 15″ × 10½″ pan (see recommendations at left)

1 pound bulk sausage

1 red bell pepper, diced

8 ounces leeks, washed and trimmed

2 tablespoons butter

1 tablespoon olive oil

1 pound mushrooms, chopped

8 ounces spinach, cooked, drained, squeezed dry, and minced

3 eggs

1 cup heavy cream

1 teaspoon dried herbes de Provence (available at specialty foods stores)

½ teaspoon salt, freshly ground pepper

½ cup parmesan cheese, freshly grated

1 teaspoon butter

1. Preheat oven to 375°.
2. Cook sausage until brown and separated into small pieces. Drain on absorbent towels and scatter on bottom of the cheese crust.
3. Drain all but 2 tablespoons of fat from the sausage pan and sauté pepper and leeks for 5 minutes. Spread over the sausage.
4. Melt 2 tablespoons butter in a skillet, add olive oil, and cook the mushrooms over moderately high heat for 8–10 minutes until the mushrooms have sweated and their juices evaporated. Sprinkle over the leeks along with the spinach.
5. Beat eggs, blend with the cream, and pour over the tart. Season with herbes de Provence, salt, and pepper. Sprinkle the parmesan evenly over the top and dot with paper-thin shavings of butter.
6. Bake at 375° for 25–30 minutes until the filling is set.

8 portions

* Extra Recipe

Joaquin's Herbed Cheese

¾ **pound cream cheese, softened**

¼ **pound chèvre cheese, softened**

¼ **pound St. André cheese, softened**

2 **cloves garlic, minced**

¾ **cup parsley, chopped**

½ **cup fresh chives, minced**
     (or 2½ tablespoons dried)

Mix all the cheeses together. Add garlic, parsley, and chives. The mixture may be molded, spread flat in pan, or rolled in a log. Refrigerate.

The herbed cheese is best when made a day ahead to allow the flavors to develop.

Yields approximately 2 cups

Joaquin Fowler

Summer Flower Arrangement
Marigolds in the Vegetable Garden

This arrangement uses materials from flower and vegetable gardens.

The components used are:

Corn
Bell peppers with fruit
Tomatoes with fruit
Squash leaves and flowers
Grapevines with grapes
Asparagus fern
White, yellow, and orange marigolds

The arrangement is done in a shallow basket lined with plastic and two pieces of soaked oasis.

Marigolds in the vegetable garden

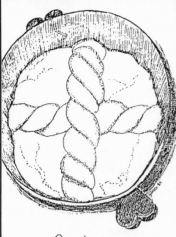

*Bread rising
in the charlotte mold*

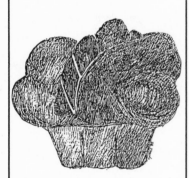

Picnic basket bread

Picnic Basket Bread

1 12-ounce can of beer

1 rounded tablespoon yeast

9 ounces warm water

6 cups unbleached flour

1 tablespoon salt

2 tablespoons herbes de Provence (available at specialty foods stores)

3 ounces country ham, minced

1 egg yolk, room temperature

1. Warm beer by running hot water over the can. In a large bowl combine yeast, beer, and water. Let sit for a few minutes until the yeast bubbles. Add 3 cups unbleached flour and mix thoroughly to form a thick paste.
2. Cover and let sit for about 8 hours until the mixture rises and falls down.
3. Add the remaining flour and the salt. Mix thoroughly and turn out on a lightly floured surface (a marble slab is best) to knead. Use a pastry scraper to keep turning the mixture until it clings together and becomes possible to knead. Pat into a circle and add the herbes de Provence and country ham. Fold the mixture in half and knead for 12–13 minutes.
4. Using ¾ of the dough, shape into a round ball and put in the bottom of a greased charlotte mold (7″ diameter, 4″ deep). Cut the remaining portion into 4 sections.
5. On the unfloured marble slab, roll 2 sections into 12″ ropes, plait them together, and place the plait across the middle of the dough in the charlotte mold, tucking the ends under. Repeat with the other 2 sections, placing the second plait perpendicular to the first. Shape leftover dough into a baguette.
6. Preheat oven to 375°.
7. Cover dough and let rise for about 40 minutes or until double. Brush with an egg yolk glaze made by whisking the yolk with 1–2 teaspoons warm water and bake at 375° for 25 minutes. Reduce the heat to 350° and bake an additional 35 minutes. (Since the baguette is smaller, bake it a total of 35 minutes.)

Yields one 7″ round loaf and one 14″ baguette

Pimiento Cheese *

This pimiento cheese was one of the staple items we packed as we headed for the beach when we were children. We thought it made *the* best sandwiches. It would make a good item for the picnic basket on another occasion.

1 5.3-ounce can evaporated milk	½ teaspoon dried mustard
1 pound sharp cheddar cheese, grated	⅛ teaspoon cayenne pepper
1 egg	⅛ teaspoon Worcestershire sauce
8 ounces pimiento, drained and finely chopped	½ teaspoon garlic salt
½ teaspoon salt	½ teaspoon onion salt

Heat the milk in the top of a double boiler, add the cheese, and stir until it has melted. Remove from the stove and add one well-beaten egg, the pimiento, and all the spices. Set aside to cool, cover, and refrigerate.

Yields approximately 3 cups

* Extra Recipe

Queen Anne's Lace arrangement

Summer Flower Arrangement
The Last Queen Anne's Lace

Queen Anne's Lace
Goldenrod
Honeysuckle
Black-eyed Susans
Native sunflower
Wild quinine
Grass
Sneezeweed

Condition the sunflower and quinine by holding 2″ of the stem end in slightly boiling water (30–60 seconds) and then letting them sit in room-temperature water for a few hours.

Plunge the rest of the flowers into room-temperature water immediately after cutting, and let them sit for 3–4 hours before arranging them.

The arrangement is done in oasis and water inside a large tin hidden in the basket. Line the basket with plastic for extra protection.

This is one of our favorite desserts. The fruit may be changed according to season availability: fresh blueberries, cherries, and cranberries are some possibilities. Fruits that discolor quickly, like peaches, apples, and bananas, may be used but must be put into the syrup at the last minute. The starfruit adds an interesting sour taste to the syrup, and its shape adds an attractive element to the compote.

Fresh Fruit with Grand Marnier Sauce

½ cup sugar

1½ cups water

1 tablespoon lemon juice

2 tablespoons Grand Marnier

2–3 oranges

3–4 kiwis

1 canteloupe

4 ounces green or black grapes

½ honeydew melon

1 pineapple

optional: 1 starfruit

1 recipe Grand Marnier Sauce

1. Make a simple syrup by dissolving the sugar in the water at a simmer. Cool. Add lemon juice and Grand Marnier.
2. Peel the oranges and kiwis and slice into crosswise pieces. Remove the rind of the canteloupe, the honeydew, and the pineapple and cut the fruit into chunks. Cut grapes in half and deseed if necessary. Add all the fruit to the syrup and chill.
3. Carry to the picnic in a large covered pitcher. Serve with the Grand Marnier sauce.

6–8 portions

Grand Marnier Sauce

This fabulous sauce keeps for 2 weeks in the refrigerator.

4–5 egg yolks

⅓ cup sugar

8 ounces heavy cream

2 tablespoons Grand Marnier

1. Place the egg yolks and sugar in the top of a double boiler or over very low heat on a gas stove. Cook slowly, stirring constantly for about 10 minutes or until the sugar has dissolved and the mixture has thickened. Set aside to cool. (The slow cooking process is important, for it allows the eggs to cook without scrambling. If the spoon picks up clumps from the bottom of the pan, the temperature is too hot.)
2. Whip cream until soft peaks form when the beater is lifted. Combine cream with yolk mixture and Grand Marnier.

Yields 2 cups

Summer Flower Arrangement
Mountain Wildflowers and Weeds

The mountains of western North Carolina abound with wildflowers and blooming weeds all summer long. In late August, flowers that have bloomed weeks earlier in the Fearrington area make a striking show in the mountains.

Components used are:

Joe-Pye weed
Goldenrod
Ironweed
Sneezeweed
Queen Anne's Lace
Snakeroot
Galax
Hydrangea
Feather bells

Put all the flowers in slightly warm water immediately after cutting to condition for 3–4 hours before being arranged. Joe-Pye weed, ironweed, and the hydrangea snowball bush should be immersed in slightly boiling water (2″ of the stem) for about 1 minute and then plunged into room-temperature water for several hours.

Mountain wildflowers and weeds

Summer Projects

1. Harvesting Herbs

2. Drying Flowers and Weeds for the Fall

3. Herb Vinegars and Oils

4. Herb Butters

5. Pesto Sauce

Harvesting Herbs

Herbs may be harvested at any time, but the best time is just before flowering, when they have increased amounts of volatile oils and are at their most flavorful and fragrant. Harvest on a dry morning just as the dew evaporates, since the sun dissipates the plants' essential oils later in the day.

Basil does not dry well; its leaves turn brown if they are even slightly bruised. But this wonderful summer annual may be used all year long in vinegars, herbed olive oils, compound butters, and pesto sauce.

Borage blossoms are perfect in summer soups. Just use them while in flower and don't try to store them.

Chives. As the flowers open, collect them and place 5–6 in the bottom of a half-pint container. Fill the container with white wine vinegar and store for several weeks. The resulting herb vinegar will be a lovely pale shade of pink.

The leaves may be frozen and used all winter as needed. They should be chopped just before using, while still in the frozen state, for they will become limp upon thawing. Our favorite herb butter combines chives, chervil, tarragon, and parsley.

Dill may be used in vinegars or frozen in the form of compound butters in combination with other herbs. Its leaves may be frozen and then chopped before thawing.

The seedheads may be harvested just as they begin to turn brown. Put the heads in a paper bag that has several slits for air circulation and hang in a warm, dry place until thoroughly dry. Shake the bag and the seeds will fall to the bottom. Store in tightly covered glass jars.

Lamb's ear dries easily by hanging in bunches upside down. At Fearrington this member of the herb family is grown for use in flower arrangements and herb wreaths. It has a wonderful gray color and a fuzzy texture that makes it an interesting contrast to notched-leaf herbs. If it is used fresh in a flower arrangement, it can be allowed to dry naturally in the moist environment and then be used all winter in other floral arrangements.

Since the lamb's ear flower is of little interest, cut the stalk just before the flower opens.

Lemon verbena keeps its bright green color the best of any dried herb. Strip the leaves from the branches before drying, since the drying process makes them brittle. We specifically dry this herb for potpourri and want it to retain its whole leaf shape.

Make a screen by removing the bottom of a produce crate and replacing it with nylon netting or hardware cloth. Using the box upside down allows air to circulate around the leaves. Scatter the leaves on top of the screen and place in a dry, dark spot. This herb dries quickly and should be ready for use in a few days.

Marjoram should be picked in the bud stage just before the flower opens. Gather the stems into a bunch, tie them with kitchen twine, and hang the bunches upside down in a dry place with good air circulation. Since the sun bleaches the color, hang marjoram in a dark place away from windows—perhaps in a kitchen corner, where a bunch of marjoram makes a nice accent. After drying, the leaves may be stripped from the branches and used in a bouquet garni.

Mint of various kinds may be hung in bunches to dry. For a faster method, dry in an oven. Set the temperature at 150°, scatter the leaves on a brown paper bag with air circulation slits in it, and place in the oven with the door ajar. The leaves are not completely dry until they may be crumbled. Allow to cool and store in a tightly covered jar.

We dry the many varieties of mint for use in the Christmas swag on the mantel. Dried mint branches thrown on a winter fire produce wonderful aromas.

Oregano is picked in full flower and hung upside down in bunches to dry. Its purple flower makes it a must for herb wreaths. The leaves can be stripped from the branches and used for bouquets garnis.

Parsley goes to flower very easily, and after it flowers the taste becomes bitter. It should accordingly be picked and used often throughout its growing season. It may be dried in the oven or frozen in combination with other herbs as a compound butter.

Pineapple sage is a fragrance herb. It produces a bright red stalky flower that also dries and may be used in potpourri. We grow this herb to garnish fruit cups and desserts and to dry for an herb swag at Christmas.

Rosemary and **sage** have such a dominating flavor that they must be used sparingly in a culinary sense. We dry them predominantly for use in herb wreaths. To harvest, take leaves and stems high on the plant, tie in bunches, and hang upside down to dry.

Sorrel has a distinctive citrus-like flavor that will be lost if it is harvested and dried. Instead put it in a skillet with butter and the water that clings to its leaves after washing. As it cooks, the leaves melt. Cool and freeze for use in soups or as a substitute for spinach.

Summer savory is one of our favorite annual herbs. We use large amounts of it while it is fresh, but find that it loses flavor as it is dried. At harvest time, it is hung upside down in bunches to dry and then used as a filler in herb wreaths.

Tarragon never comes into flower in our garden because it is cut and used so frequently in its fresh state. We harvest it for herb vinegars in June, when the stalks are tender. In combination with parsley, chives, and chervil it makes a Fines Herbes butter, which should be frozen.

Thyme. The whole family of thymes is dried by hanging in bunches or by being spread on screens (see Lemon Verbena, above). In its dried form we use it in bouquets garnis or in herb wreaths.

Drying Flowers and Weeds for the Fall

Glycerine

The glycerine method of drying and preserving foliage should be used in the summer, when plant material seems to absorb the liquid more rapidly. The glycerine is purchased from the pharmacy and diluted: 1 part glycerine to 2 parts water. Fill a glass container with about 6 inches of the solution and stand stems upright. Leaves react differently by changing color. Magnolia turns a wonderful shade of satin brown; elaeagnus may turn yellow. Completely immerse ivy leaves in the solution.

Aspidistra	**English ivy**	**Magnolia**
Elaeagnus	**Galax**	

Natural Drying

In this method, one simply collects from nature as flowerheads become brown pods or as material dries in the garden at the end of the season, such as okra. Moss may be collected at any season and stays green indefinitely. Artichokes and pomegranates may be purchased and left sitting in a basket to dry.

Artichoke	**Magnolia and magnolia pods**	**Poppy pods**
Cotton balls		**Rose of Sharon**
Dock	**Milkweed pods**	**Sea oats**
Empress tree pods	**Moss**	**Sedum Autumn Joy**
Iris pods	**Okra**	
Juniper	**Pomegranate**	**Trumpet vine**

Pressing

Dried materials that have been pressed retain their colors very well. Lay newspapers on the floor of a warm, dry place. Being careful not to let leaves touch (or they may stick together), place the foliage on the newspapers. Cover with another layer of newspapers, and weight with bricks or heavy wood. Several layers may be dried at one time by using sheets of plywood between the layers and weighting with heavy bricks on the top layer.

Ferns	**Grass**	**Leaves**

Sand

Flowers dried in sand retain both their shape and their color. The sand is spread 2″ deep in the bottom of a box or carton. Strip the foliage from the stem, leaving 1″–2″ of stem intact, and place the flowerhead face down in the sand. Gently cover the flowers completely with sand and store in a dark, cool place. Flowers should occasionally be removed to check the drying process, which generally takes from one to three weeks.

Dogwood, pink	Marigold	Zinnia
Lily-of-the-valley	Rose	

Silica Gel

Silica gel is a dehydrating agent packaged and sold in garden centers under the name Flower-Dri. It may be used over and over and simply needs to be dried in an oven to be returned to its usable state. In this method flowerheads are placed face up in a container, gently covered with the silica gel, and sealed in the container. Most materials dry within four to seven days, but flowers should be checked during the drying process to make certain they have not become brittle.

The list of flowers and foliage that can be dried by this method is endless.

Ageratum	Delphinium	Marigold
Aster	Dogwood	Pansy
Baby's breath	Dusty miller	Peony
Bells of Ireland	Foxglove	Rose
Calendula	Gardenia	Sage
Carnation	Gladiolus	Snapdragon
Chrysanthemum	Hyacinth	Spirea
Columbine	Ivy leaves	Stock
Cornflower	Lamb's ear	Viola
Dahlia	Larkspur	Zinnia
Daisy	Lavender	

Upright-in-Water

The upright-in-water method simply means that the flowers are used in an arrangement, dry by themselves naturally, and then are stored for use another time in their dried state.

Boxwood	Joe-Pye weed
Corn	Polygonum
Deodora	Queen Anne's Lace
Elderberry	Sorghum
Goldenrod	Sourwood
Holly	Statice
Hydrangea	Yarrow

Upside Down

The hanging method for drying flowers is the easiest and the one most often used. After foliage is stripped from the stems, the stems are tied together in groups of ten or so (unless the flowerheads are extremely large) and hung head down in a dry, dark place.

Artemesia Silver King	Pokeberry
Bittersweet	Rabbit tobacco
Cattails	Scotch broom
Cockscomb	Strawflowers
Dusty miller	Sumac
Herbs	Sunflowers
Onion and leek flowerheads	

Herb Vinegars and Oils

Herb vinegars are easy to make and rewarding to use, especially in the dead of winter when fresh herbs are hard to come by.

The following are some general guidelines for making herb vinegar of any kind:

1. Gather herbs in mid-morning after the dew has evaporated. The volatile oils are at their peak at this time of day.
2. If it is necessary to wash the herbs to remove grit, be certain they are absolutely dry before combining with the vinegar.
3. Always make the vinegars in glass jars with non-metal tops. A metal top may cause a reaction between the vinegar and the metal.
4. Use a good-quality vinegar. An inferior vinegar will produce an herb vinegar of the same quality.
5. Heat the vinegar, but do not boil. The warming procedure helps hasten infusion with the herbs.

Basil and garlic teamed with a red wine vinegar make an especially nice herb vinegar to use in vinaigrettes. Spear two garlic cloves on a toothpick and place them in the bottom of a half-pint glass container along with three 4″ pieces of basil. Gently fill the container with the heated vinegar, using a funnel. Seal it and place it in a dark, dry place for at least a month for the flavor to develop. This variety has the most distinctive aroma when uncapped.

Basil-garlic olive oil. Put 2–3 garlic cloves on a toothpick and place them in the bottom of a half-pint glass container. Push 3 sprigs of basil into the jar and fill the container with a good-quality olive oil. Set in a dark place for a couple of months to let the flavors develop. Strain through double layers of cheesecloth before use. To uncork the container is to smell the essence of summer.

Chive blossoms produce a vinegar with a soft pink color. Place 5–6 blossom heads in the bottom of a half-pint glass container, fill the container with heated white wine vinegar, seal it, and store as above.

Tarragon vinegar is useful for salad vinaigrettes and for helping produce a more flavorful béarnaise sauce. Use three 4″ sprigs per half-pint container. Fill the container with heated white wine vinegar, seal it, and set it aside for flavors to develop.

A basket with all three vinegars would be an especially welcome gift for cooks.

Herb Butters

Basil Butter

1 stick butter, softened

1 teaspoon lemon juice

1 shallot, minced

1 clove garlic, minced

2 tablespoons fresh basil, minced

Combine seasonings with the softened butter, shape into a log, and refrigerate until slightly firm. Smooth the edges, wrap in wax paper, and freeze.

Chive Butter

1 stick butter, softened

1 tablespoon parsley, minced

1 tablespoon chives, minced

2 teaspoons lemon juice

2–3 teaspoons shallots, minced

⅛ teaspoon salt, freshly ground white pepper

Mix all ingredients. Use wax paper to roll into a log shape. Refrigerate or freeze.

Fines Herbes Butter

1 stick butter, softened

2 teaspoons tarragon wine vinegar

1 shallot, minced

2 teaspoons fresh parsley, minced

2 teaspoons fresh chives, minced

2 teaspoons fresh tarragon, minced

2 teaspoons fresh chervil, minced

⅛ teaspoon salt, freshly ground pepper

Combine all ingredients. Chill until ready to use or freeze.

Green Peppercorn Butter

4 ounces butter, softened

2 tablespoons green peppercorns, drained and rinsed

1 tablespoon lemon juice

¼ teaspoon salt

1 tablespoon shallots, minced

1 tablespoon dijon mustard

1 tablespoon parsley, minced

Mix all ingredients together and shape into a log. Refrigerate or freeze.

Lemon Herb Butter

1 stick butter, softened

2 tablespoons lemon juice

1 tablespoon parsley, minced

2 tablespoons chives, minced

1 tablespoon scallions, minced

Combine all ingredients, shape into a log, fill a crock, pack into a hollowed vegetable, or freeze.

Tarragon Butter

1 stick butter, softened

2 teaspoons tarragon vinegar

1 teaspoon scallions, minced

2 teaspoons fresh tarragon, minced

1 tablespoon fresh parsley, chopped

¼ teaspoon pepper, freshly ground

Fluff the butter by beating it in a small bowl with a wooden spoon. Add all the ingredients and shape into a log or crock. May be chilled or frozen for later use.

Any herbed butter can be spread to a ½″ thickness in a large pan. Refrigerate until the butter is firm, and then use cookie cutters to cut the butter into shapes, which can be put into a bowl of cold water until ready to use.

Pesto Sauce

Nothing celebrates summer and herbs any better than pesto. To stash away an abundance of basil for use during the winter is the best thing an herb gardener can do. We grow both bush basil and the larger, leafed variety in enough quantity to use in the Fearrington House kitchen almost daily. By midsummer the plants have grown to a huge size and it is time to harvest. The pesto is divided into small containers and frozen.

Our recipe for pesto is an adaptation from Giuliano Bugialli, an Italian cookbook author and teacher. The multiple varieties of greens, cheeses, and nuts produce *the* most delicious sauce.

½ cup parmesan cheese

¼ cup Romano cheese

¼ pound country ham

1½ cups olive oil

3–3½ cups fresh basil leaves

¼ cup spinach, boiled, squeezed dry, and minced

2 tablespoons pecans

2 tablespoons pine nuts

3 cloves garlic

½ teaspoon salt, freshly ground pepper

Grate the cheeses in the work bowl of a food processor, remove, and set aside. Shred the country ham in the food processor, remove, and set aside.

Place ½ cup olive oil in the food processor container and begin adding the rest of the ingredients. Process until the mixture is finely ground. Add the remaining olive oil and blend until smooth.

Package in 4-ounce containers with lids and freeze.

AUTUMN

After the Game

Cream of Vidalia Onion Soup

*   *   *

Filet Mignon with Green Peppercorn Sauce

Grits Timbale

Green Beans and Wax Beans with Bread Crumbs

Sautéed Button Mushrooms with Brandy

*   *   *

Fearrington House Bourbon Pecan Pie

Serves 8–10 people

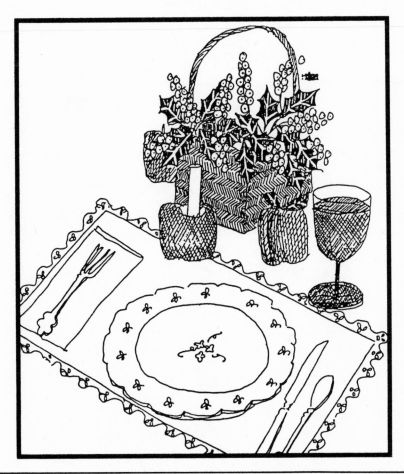

Cream of Vidalia Onion Soup

¼ pound bacon, cut into ½″ strips

1 stick unsalted butter

3 pounds Vidalia onions, peeled and
  thinly sliced

8 cloves garlic, peeled and left whole

2 cups dry white wine

1 quart chicken stock

1 bay leaf

1 tablespoon fresh thyme (or 1 teaspoon
  dried thyme)

1 cup heavy cream

1 cup crème fraiche or sour cream

3 tablespoons lemon juice

½ teaspoon salt, freshly ground white pepper

Tabasco and nutmeg to taste

2 cups homemade croutons

1 cup scallions, sliced

1. In a large Dutch oven, cook bacon slowly until crisp. Remove
   and reserve. Add butter, onions, and garlic cloves to bacon
   renderings, cover, and cook over low heat, stirring often, until
   onions are translucent and lightly caramelized. Add wine, stock,
   bay leaf, and thyme, bring to a boil, and simmer 30 minutes.
2. Strain the soup mixture, remove bay leaf, and process solids in
   a food processor with a steel knife. Pass soup through the fine
   blade of a food mill. Combine the two mixtures and chill.
3. Whisk in cream and crème fraiche. Season with lemon juice,
   salt, pepper, Tabasco, and nutmeg.
4. Serve in chilled bowls. Garnish with crisp bacon, croutons, and
   scallions.

8 portions

Ben Barker

Autumn Flower Arrangement
Mostly Dried Weeds

The arrangement is done in a basket containing two blocks of dry oasis and rocks. Rocks are necessary because the arrangement contains so much material that it is topheavy.

The elements of the arrangement are gathered in the summer months and dried individually. (See pp. 132–34 for instructions and methods of drying.) Some have previously been used in flower arrangements, dried during that time, and were saved for later use.

Components of the arrangement are:

Cattails
Dock
Feather grass
Goldenrod
Grasses
Leaves
Queen Anne's Lace
Rabbit tobacco
Sedum
Siberian iris pods
Sorghum
Sumac
Yarrow

Green Peppercorn Sauce

This recipe as an accompaniment to filet mignon goes equally well with roast loin, eye of the round, whole tenderloin, or steak.

> ½ cup beef bouillon
>
> 2 garlic cloves, minced
>
> 2 tablespoons butter
>
> 3–4 tablespoons red wine vinegar
>
> 2 tablespoons sherry
>
> 4 tablespoons green peppercorns, rinsed and drained
>
> 2 teaspoons dried thyme
>
> ¼ teaspoon salt, freshly ground pepper
>
> ½ pint heavy cream

1. Bring the beef bouillon to a boil and cook until reduced by half.
2. Sauté garlic in butter over moderate heat. Blend in reduced beef bouillon, wine vinegar, and sherry. Reduce by half.
3. Add peppercorns, thyme, salt, and pepper to taste. Add heavy cream and cook until slightly thickened.

Yields approximately 1 cup

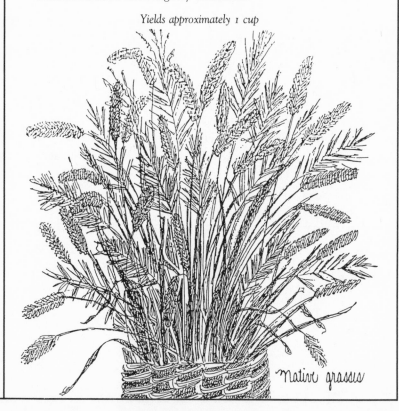

native grasses

Grits Timbale

This flavorful timbale could easily take the place of the confetti rice in the Christmas dinner menu. Here a food staple long associated with the South is presented in an unexpected manner.

6 cups water

1½ cups grits

2 teaspoons salt

2 cloves garlic, minced

1½ cups medium-sharp cheddar cheese, grated

2 tablespoons parmesan cheese, freshly grated

3 egg yolks

⅓ cup heavy cream

½ teaspoon salt, freshly ground black pepper

1. Preheat oven to 350°.
2. Bring water to a boil in a medium saucepan and add grits and salt. Cook according to package directions until the mass has thickened.
3. Remove from heat and blend in the garlic, cheeses, egg yolks, heavy cream, salt, and pepper.
4. Fill twelve 4-ounce buttered ramekins ¾ full and place in a baking dish large enough to accommodate all 12. Add hot—almost boiling—water to the baking dish until it is halfway up the sides of the ramekins. Cover the baking dish with foil and bake at 350° for ½ hour.
5. Remove from the oven and let cool in the baking dish. Run a knife around the edge of each ramekin, turn upside down, and lightly tap to release the timbale from the baking dish.

12 portions

Changing the Timbale

The grits timbale would be quite nice with a layer of spinach, carrots, or red bell pepper placed on the bottom of the ramekin before filling with the grits mixture.

An addition of minced sautéed mushrooms and scallions plus ¼ cup freshly grated parmesan cheese sprinkled over the unmolded timbale and served with a Mornay sauce could turn the timbale into a very special first course.

Autumn Flower Arrangement

Pumpkin and Vegetables

The components of this arrangement are:

Medium-sized pumpkin
Green grapes
Leaves
Lilies
Goldenrod
Ivy
3–5 fresh artichokes
Small gourds
Pomegranates

Work on this arrangement must begin several days before it is put together. Cut the top from the pumpkin, scoop out the seeds and part of the pulp, and set outside to dry in the air for several days.

Leaves, lilies, goldenrod, and ivy are arranged in soaked oasis in a container set inside the pumpkin. Balance the grapes over the edge of the pumpkin.

Push strong heavy wire into the base of the artichokes, gourds, and pomegranates so that they can be placed in the arrangement and bent into place. If heavy wire is unavailable, use a stick or plant stake cut to the appropriate length.

Green Beans and Wax Beans with Bread Crumbs

2 slices good-quality bread

1 pound green beans

1 pound fresh wax beans

1 ounce butter

2 cloves garlic, minced

1. Remove crusts from bread and make crumbs by rolling pieces between the palms of the hands. Set aside.
2. Wash and string both varieties of beans.
3. Bring water to a boil in a large stockpot and cook beans for about 2 minutes. Drain and refresh with cold water to set the bright green color.
4. Melt the butter in a heavy skillet and lightly brown the garlic over medium heat. Add the beans and bread crumbs, raise the heat slightly, and stir for 2–3 minutes until the bread crumbs have browned.

8 portions

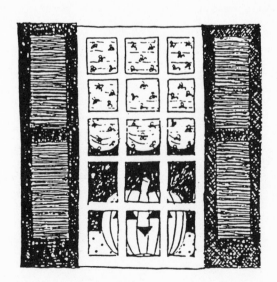

Sautéed Button Mushrooms with Brandy

1½ pounds fresh mushrooms

½ cup soft bread crumbs

2 tablespoons butter

2 cloves garlic, minced

1 tablespoon lemon juice

1½ tablespoons brandy

½ cup heavy cream

1 cup parmesan cheese, freshly grated

1. Wipe the mushrooms with a damp paper towel to clean. Remove stems and reserve for another use.
2. Remove crusts from good-quality bread and roll pieces between the palms of the hand to make bread crumbs (the food processor makes too fine a crumb). Toast until golden brown and set aside.
3. Melt the butter in a large skillet and add the mushroom caps and minced garlic. Drizzle with lemon juice and cook over medium high heat, rolling the mushrooms in the pan to cook evenly. Add brandy. After 5–10 minutes pour in the heavy cream and reduce slightly.
4. To serve, sprinkle with parmesan cheese and toasted bread crumbs.

8 portions

*This recipe for pie filling
will make 4 dozen 2″ tarts.
Preheat oven to 375°. Double
the ingredients for cream
cheese pastry (below) and
press into the bottom of well-
greased muffin tin cups. Scatter pecans over the pastry,
ladle filling over the pecans,
and bake for about 20 minutes or until filling is golden
brown and set.*

Cream Cheese Pastry

*This cream cheese pastry is
quick and easy. It is perfect
for individual sweet tarts or
for hors d'oeuvres cases. Scatter chopped spinach, to-
matoes, ham, or bacon over
the pastry, fill with a tablespoon of quiche mixture, and
bake until set.*

**1 stick butter
1 cup unbleached flour
3 ounces cream cheese**

*Mix all the ingredients to-
gether and chill. Pinch off a
small amount of dough, roll
into a ball, and press into a
well-greased muffin tin cup.
Flatten with fingers to cover
the bottom and sides. Fill and
bake at 375°.*

*The dough may be rolled,
but must be well chilled.*

*Yields approximately 2 dozen
2″ shells*

Fearrington House Bourbon Pecan Pie

From the early days of Fearrington House, this pie has been the favorite. People have even asked to purchase a whole one to take home.

The pie may be made in a 9″ pie pan, or as individual 4″ tarts baked with a whole pecan in the center.

1 9″ pie shell, partially baked (recipe p. 100)

⅓ cup butter, melted

1 cup firmly packed brown sugar

3 eggs

1 tablespoon bourbon

½ cup light corn syrup

½ teaspoon salt

1 cup pecans, chopped

½ pint heavy cream, whipped

1. Preheat oven to 375°.
2. Combine butter and sugar in a mixer. Add eggs one at a time, beating well. Stir in bourbon, corn syrup, salt, and pecans.
3. Pour into pie shell and bake at 375° for about 45 minutes or until a knife inserted in the middle comes out clean.
4. Serve with freshly whipped cream or homemade vanilla ice cream.

6–8 portions

Pig Pickin' in the Barn

Pork Barbeque, Whole Meat and Chopped

Robert's Barbeque Sauce

Brunswick Stew

Baked Beans

Skillet Potatoes with Scallions and Chives

Three-Cabbage Slaw

Hush Puppies

*   *   *

Country Apple Tart with Lemon Zest and
Vanilla Ice Cream

Serves 25 people

Fire barrel

Pig Pickin' Barbeque

This old-fashioned hickory barbeque takes dedicated people to execute, since the total preparation time can be as much as 15–18 hours. It is a fascinating procedure. Hickory is used for the cooking because it is hard and imparts flavor in the cooking process. If possible, the wood should be freshly cut, split, and stacked to await the pig pickin'.

The pigs should weigh 110–130 pounds; meat from a pig of this size will cook better and be more tender than meat from a larger pig. Barbeque pigs may be ordered from a local sausage company; they will dress the meat and perhaps deliver it. Half a pig serves 25 people.

The cooking begins the day before the party. To make the coals, hickory logs are stacked in a fire barrel, which is a 55-gallon drum with a rack. The wood is set afire and burns for about an hour. As the fire burns, the coals drop through the rack to the bottom. When the coals are 12″ deep they can be gathered from the bottom and shoveled into the grill to lightly cover the surface of the cooker. The fire barrel is used all night long, since fresh coals must be added every 20–30 minutes to assure uniform cooking. Coals are added by the half shovelful. There must be a balance between adding too many coals, which would burn the meat, and adding enough to keep the fire going.

In the larger cookers the grill is 14″ above the coals. The quarters are placed on the grill cut side down so that the fat slowly drips out during the cooking process (otherwise the meat would be very greasy). After 8–10 hours the meat is turned and the skin side goes down. The meat now begins to baste itself and will cook about another 5 hours before being ready.

At the end of the cooking process the joints in the shoulder move easily and the skin begins to separate from the meat. In effect, an air pocket forms that can be felt when the meat is pressed with a finger. In another test for doneness the shoulder blade pops out easily when pulled. A final test would be inserting an instant meat thermometer; it should read 170°. Once the correct temperature is reached, remove the meat from the grill to the chopping block. At this point there is so much internal heat that the meat would turn dark and become dry if allowed to stay on the grill.

In traditional pig pickin' the meat is left whole and people remove what they wish.

If the meat is to be chopped, it is removed in chunks and cleaned of its fat before being chopped. (This important step is overlooked by most people who prepare barbeque.) During the chopping the tenderloin pieces are left in larger chunks, since they are already tender. The skin from the rib cage, called the crackling, is especially tasty when finely minced and mixed with the other meat.

To mix with sauce, use 3 quarts sauce for each whole pig.

Variation: Squirrel or rabbit may be added to the other meats for a more authentic down-home Brunswick stew.

Robert's Barbeque Sauce

1 quart white vinegar	2 tablespoons lemon juice
½ cup sugar	¼ ounce pepper
1 cup brown sugar	¼ ounce ground red pepper
16 ounces ketchup	1½ teaspoons hot sauce
2 tablespoons Worcestershire sauce	1 tablespoon salt

Combine all ingredients except ketchup in a stockpot and bring to a boil. Cook over medium heat, stirring occasionally until the sugar is dissolved. Add ketchup at the end to keep from scorching.

Yields approximately 1½ quarts

Brunswick Stew

3 pounds beef, cut for stewing

3 pounds pork, cut for stewing

1 hen, 4–5 pounds, cut up

½ teaspoon salt, freshly ground pepper

4 cups canned tomatoes

2 cups fresh corn

1 quart butter beans, shelled

2 pounds fresh or frozen okra, sliced

2 large onions, chopped

15 medium-size white potatoes, peeled and chopped

1. Place the beef, pork, and chicken in a large kettle or Dutch oven with just enough water to cover, and bring to a boil. Cover and simmer gently about 2 hours until tender.
2. Cool. Remove bone and skin from the chicken, and return the chicken meat to the broth. Skim the fat from the top.
3. Add remaining ingredients (including more water if necessary) and simmer until meat cooks to shreds. Taste for seasoning.

25–30 portions

Baked Beans

1 2-quart bean pot

2 pounds dried beans (preferably California pea beans)

1 pound salt pork

1 medium-size onion

½ cup sugar

⅔ cup molasses

2 teaspoons dry mustard

4 teaspoons salt

½ teaspoon freshly ground pepper

The bean pot, a special earthenware shaped pot with a lid, is traditionally used just for baking beans. The beans are layered between two pieces of salt pork and cooked in a medium slow oven for a long time. It is necessary to check the beans several times as they cook, since they absorb water readily and more liquid may need to be added.

1. Pick over the beans by the handful and discard the darkened ones. Cover with cold water in a large pot and soak overnight. Drain and rinse with cold water.
2. Preheat oven to 300°.
3. Dice the salt pork into ½″ squares. Put half on the bottom of the bean pot with a whole onion (not sliced). Add all the beans and then the remaining salt pork.
4. Mix the other ingredients with enough hot water to cover the beans. Bake at 300° for 6 hours, adding hot water as necessary to keep the beans moist.

25 portions

Nell Elder

Skillet Potatoes with Scallions and Chives

6 pounds small red potatoes

6 ounces butter

⅓ cup olive oil

1½ cups scallions, minced

½ cup chives, minced

1½ teaspoons dried thyme

½ teaspoon salt, freshly ground pepper

1. Parboil the red potatoes for about 12 minutes. Drain, cool, and cut into quarters.
2. Heat butter and olive oil in a large skillet. Cook potatoes over moderate heat for about 8 minutes. Add scallions, chives, thyme, salt, and pepper. Cook 2 more minutes or until potatoes are golden brown.

25 portions

Three-Cabbage Slaw

3 pounds red cabbage

3 pounds green cabbage

3 pounds savoy cabbage

⅓ cup red wine vinegar

1½ cups mayonnaise

⅔ cup scallions, chopped

2 teaspoons Worcestershire sauce

2 tablespoons salt

¼ cup sugar

¼ cup ketchup

⅓ cup celery seed

¼ cup dijon mustard

1. Cut the cabbage in half and then in small wedges. With the steel blade in place in a food processor, shred the cabbage with quick on and off turns.
2. Place in a large bowl and add vinegar, mayonnaise, and remaining ingredients. Mix well and chill.

25 portions

Hush Puppies

¾ cup unbleached flour

1 tablespoon baking powder

1½ teaspoons salt

1 teaspoon sugar

1½ cups cornmeal

2 eggs, beaten

⅓ cup milk

1¼ cups water

1 tablespoon oil

2 tablespoons onion, minced

¼ cup scallions, minced

vegetable oil for frying

1. Sift the flour, baking powder, salt, and sugar together.
2. Combine the cornmeal, eggs, milk, and water. Blend with the dry ingredients, oil, onion, and scallions.
3. Drop by the teaspoonful into hot (375°) vegetable oil that is about 1″ deep in the skillet. Fry until golden. Drain on absorbent towels.

Yields approximately 3 dozen

Country Apple Tart
with Lemon Zest
and Vanilla Ice Cream

This is the simplest possible tart, and one of the best. Be sure to use a cooking apple such as Granny Smith, Winesap, or McIntosh. Keep the vanilla ice cream in a bucket surrounded by ice so that guests may help themselves when it's time for dessert.

1 recipe All-Purpose Pastry (p. 53)

¼ cup apricot preserves

2 tablespoons sugar

5–6 apples

½ cup sugar

1 teaspoon cinnamon

freshly grated nutmeg

2 lemon rinds, finely grated

2 tablespoons butter

1 quart vanilla ice cream

1. Preheat oven to 400°.
2. Roll out pastry to fit a 12″ × 16″ pan. Sprinkle a cookie sheet with cold water before putting pastry in place to help keep it from shrinking. Fold in the edges ⅜″ to make a flat rim. Dock the edge with a knife to make a decorative mark all the way around (do not cut all the way through the pastry).
3. Heat apricot preserves in a saucepan and brush over surface of pastry. Sprinkle with 2 tablespoons sugar.
4. Peel and core apples and slice them very thin (⅛″). Arrange in a pattern. Sprinkle again with sugar, lemon rind, nutmeg, and cinnamon.
5. Dot with paper-thin pieces of butter. Bake at 400° for 25 minutes.
6. Cut into rectangles roughly 2½″ × 2″ and serve with ice cream.

Yields 30 small portions

Autumn Flower Arrangement
Sumac, Knotweed, and Sourwood

This arrangement can become almost a permanent one for fall.

Cut the knotweed in the summer when it is at the peak of its bloom. Remove leaves individually up and down the stem; place the branches in water and leave them to dry for a week or so in a spot where they will be undisturbed.

Gather the sumac in early September, when the fruit is bright red. Remove the leaves and set the branches aside to dry for several days. As the fruit dries its color will darken somewhat, but it will remain for several seasons if the branches are stored in a dry place.

All the branches are placed in soaked oasis in a container set inside a basket. The sourwood leaves are the only component needing moisture; they may be left in the arrangement to dry naturally as the moisture in the oasis decreases.

All plant material is a dark fall shade of red.

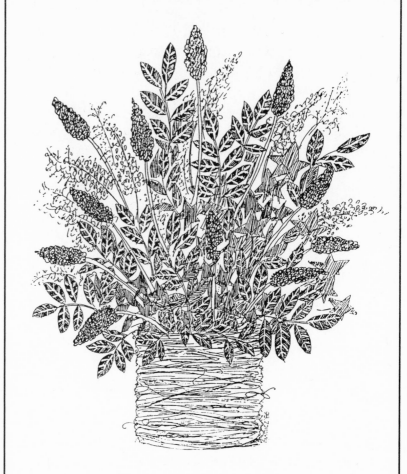

Sumac, knotweed, sourwood

In Celebration of Fall

Mushroom Roll with Red Bell Pepper Mayonnaise

*   *   *

Veal Loin Roast

Swiss Chard with Pecans

Steamed Matchstick Carrots and Celery

Eggplant and Zucchini Stuffed with
Rice and Tomatoes

Monkey Bread

*   *   *

Poached Pears with Raspberry Sauce and
Chocolate Curls

Serves 6–8 people

Vidalia Onion Cups
with Black-eyed Peas *

1 pound dried black-eyed peas

6 medium-size onions, preferably Vidalia onions

2 teaspoons butter

¼ teaspoon salt, freshly ground pepper

4 ounces bacon, fried until crisp and chopped

4 tablespoons olive oil

2½ cups onion, chopped

3 cloves garlic

½ teaspoon salt, freshly ground pepper

1½ teaspoons dried herbes de Provence
   (available at specialty foods stores)

5 fresh tomatoes, peeled, seeded, and chopped

1. Soak peas overnight in a large bowl with water completely covering the peas. Drain the next day and set aside.
2. Preheat oven to 375°.
3. Cut a slice from the top of each onion and remove the center
   with a melon ball scooper, leaving a ¼″ wall. Measure the pulp
   and set aside to use in flavoring the peas.
4. Arrange the onions in a baking pan and place a pat of butter in
   the center of each. Cover with foil and bake at 375° for 40–60
   minutes.
5. Heat olive oil and 2 tablespoons bacon drippings in a large
   enamel skillet. Over medium heat sauté chopped onions and
   garlic for 8–10 minutes until translucent but not browned. Add
   the black-eyed peas, salt, pepper, and herbes de Provence, and
   enough water to cover the peas completely. Cover the saucepan
   and simmer very slowly for 40–45 minutes. Add tomatoes 15
   minutes before end of cooking time so that they will not disintegrate. Check to see if more water should be added during cooking time. At the end, water should be almost absorbed and peas
   tender. Taste for salt and pepper.
6. Divide the peas among the onion cups and sprinkle with bacon.
   The onion cups may be reheated at 250° for a few minutes if
   necessary.

6 portions

* Extra Recipe

Mushroom Roll with Red Bell Pepper Mayonnaise

1 tablespoon vegetable oil
(to oil the pan)

2 tablespoons butter

1 medium-size onion,
finely chopped

1 clove garlic, minced

2 10-ounce packages frozen
spinach, cooked, drained,
squeezed dry, and minced

freshly grated nutmeg

½ teaspoon salt,
freshly ground white pepper

2–3 tablespoons parmesan
cheese, freshly grated

2 tablespoons heavy cream

1 pound mushrooms

6 eggs, separated

4 ounces butter, melted

½ teaspoon salt,
freshly ground pepper

2 tablespoons lemon juice

2 tablespoons parsley, minced

1 teaspoon chives, minced

1 recipe Red Bell Pepper
Mayonnaise

*The mushroom roll may be
served warm or cold and may
be prepared in advance and
reheated.*

*For a slightly more time-
consuming preparation, sauté
button mushrooms (recipe
p. 147) to garnish the mushroom roll in addition to the
red bell pepper mayonnaise.*

1. Preheat oven to 375°.
2. Grease a jelly roll pan (15″ × 10½″). Line with parchment
   paper and grease the paper.
3. Melt the butter in a heavy skillet, and cook the onion and garlic
   over medium heat for about 10 minutes until they are translucent but not browned. Remove the pan from the heat and
   add the spinach, nutmeg, salt, pepper, parmesan, and heavy
   cream. Scatter evenly over the bottom of the paper-lined jelly
   roll pan.
4. Wipe the mushrooms clean with a damp cloth, chop finely, and
   working in small amounts, wring them dry in the corner of a
   towel. Beat the egg yolks and combine them with the mushrooms, butter, salt, pepper, and lemon juice. Beat the egg whites
   until soft peaks form. Quickly fold in the mushroom mixture
   and spread on top of the spinach in the jelly roll pan.
5. Bake at 375° for 20 minutes or until set. Remove from the oven
   and invert on a dampened towel. Peel the parchment paper
   away and use the towel to roll the mushrooms into a log shape.
   Lift the roll and place seam side down on a serving platter. Slice
   and serve immediately with parsley, chives, and red bell pepper
   mayonnaise.

8–10 portions

The peppers may be roasted in the oven by arranging them in a pan and setting them under the broiler. Turn each one until all the skin is blistered and blackened.

Red Bell Pepper Mayonnaise

2 red bell peppers

2 egg yolks

3 cloves garlic, minced

2 tablespoons lemon juice

1 teaspoon salt, freshly ground white pepper

1–1½ cups olive oil

1. Roast the peppers by putting them on an open flame on a gas range. Holding the peppers with a long-handled fork, char and blister each one completely. Place in a brown paper bag until cooled. Peel each pepper, deseed, cut into pieces, and purée in a blender or food processor. Remove and set aside.
2. Put the yolks in the bottom of a blender and add the garlic, lemon juice, salt, and freshly ground pepper. Blend for a few seconds and begin adding oil drop by drop from a baster. After ¾ of the oil has been blended and the sauce is beginning to thicken, add the rest of the oil in a slow, steady stream.
3. Blend in the puréed peppers.

Yields 1½–2 cups mayonnaise

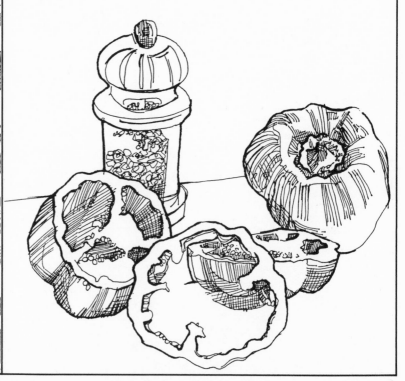

Creasie Green Soup[*]

Creasie greens grow wild in the South. They are in season in the fall and sometimes may even be found in the grocery store. Another time substitute this humble but elegant soup in the autumn menu.

2 cups creasie greens

1 cup romaine lettuce

1 cup spinach

2 tablespoons butter

1 large onion or 3 leeks, chopped

1½ quarts chicken stock

2 potatoes, peeled and chopped

½ teaspoon salt, freshly ground pepper

1 cup heavy cream

1. Wash and drain the greens. Bunch the greens into a single pile, hold tightly, slice into thin pieces, and set aside.
2. Melt the butter and cook the onion over medium heat for about 10 minutes until it is softened and translucent but not browned.
3. Add the chicken stock, potatoes, salt, and pepper and bring to a boil. Simmer about 20 minutes until potatoes are tender.
4. Blend in the greens and cook 5 more minutes. Purée and add heavy cream. May be served warm or cool.

6–8 portions

* Extra Recipe

Medallions of Pork

Another time substitute this elegant pork tenderloin for the veal loin roast in the menu.

The sauce (minus the butter) must be ready before cooking the meat and may be done earlier in the day. Use only pork tenderloins that are available at better grocery stores and butcher shops.

3 pounds pork tenderloin, cut into 2-ounce portions

1 tablespoon corn oil

3 cups chicken stock

1 rounded tablespoon tomato paste

2 ounces clarified butter

2 cups white wine

2 tablespoons butter, room temperature

1. Begin the sauce early in the day by simmering the chicken stock.

2. Caramelize the tomato paste in clarified butter until it is very dark, stirring frequently.

3. Reduce the white wine to about ½ cup. Combine with tomato paste and ½ cup chicken stock. Simmer for 10 minutes, strain, and set aside.

4. Preheat oven to 425°.

5. In a large sauté pan heat corn oil until it is very hot (almost smoking). Place the medallions in the pan and sear ½–2 minutes. Using tongs and a spatula together, quickly turn each medallion and place the whole pan in the preheated oven. Bake 8–10 minutes. An internal thermometer should register 150°.

(Continued on pg. 163)

Veal Loin Roast

This roast makes an elegant though expensive meal. Allow ½ pound of meat per person and then a little extra just to be certain.

The roast may be stuffed with sprigs of fresh thyme and marjoram if you have the butcher put the herbs inside before it is tied.

1 tablespoon butter

1 tablespoon olive oil

3½–4 pounds veal loin (center cut)

½ cup chicken stock

1 bouquet garni (thyme, oregano, bay leaf, and parsley)

½ teaspoon salt, freshly ground white pepper

⅓ cup white wine

2 tablespoons flour

8 ounces heavy cream

1 bunch fresh parsley, minced

1. Preheat oven to 325°.
2. Melt the butter and add the olive oil in a heavy roasting pan. Brown the veal thoroughly. Add the chicken stock, salt, pepper, and bouquet garni.
3. Cover and roast at 325° for about 2 hours (allow 25–30 minutes cooking time per pound), basting often. The veal is cooked when an instant thermometer reads 175°.
4. Remove the veal from the pan and degrease the pan with white wine. Remove and set aside all but 2 tablespoons of stock from the pan. Add flour to the stock and cook, stirring constantly, for 2 minutes. Strain the set-aside juices and slowly add back to the flour-stock mixture, whisking slowly until thickened. Add salt, pepper, and heavy cream. Heat through.
5. Slice the roast and arrange slices in an overlapping fashion on the serving plate. Nap with the sauce and garnish with minced parsley.

6–8 portions

Swiss Chard with Pecans

3 tablespoons pecans, chopped

3 tablespoons unsalted butter

3 pounds fresh Swiss chard

freshly grated nutmeg

¼ teaspoon salt, freshly ground pepper

1. In a small skillet, sauté the pecans in 1 tablespoon butter over moderate heat until they are golden. Set aside to drain on absorbent towels.
2. Wash the Swiss chard well to remove any possible grit. Remove the coarse main stem.
3. In a large skillet, cook the Swiss chard over moderately high heat in the water that clings to the leaves after washing. When the chard wilts, add the remaining butter, the pecans, and a grating of fresh nutmeg. Heat through, add salt and pepper, and serve.

6–8 portions

6. *While the medallions are roasting, reheat the sauce almost to a simmer.*

7. *Remove meat from the oven and arrange on a serving platter. Take sauce from the heat and swirl in 2 tablespoons of butter. Pour over the meat and serve immediately.*

8 portions

Cory Mattson

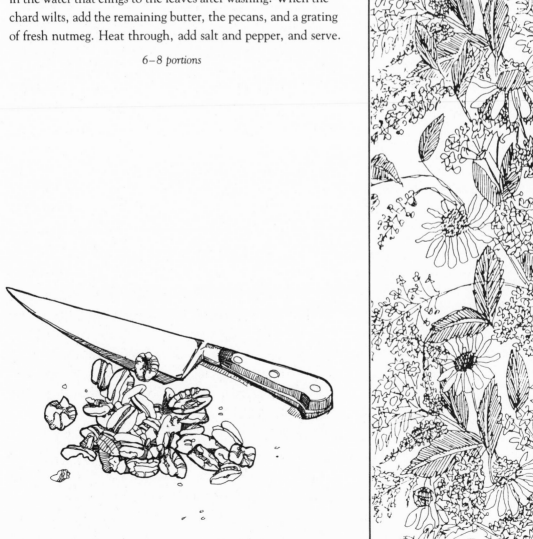

In the summertime, when tomatoes taste as they should, they too can be used as shells for this recipe. Cut a slice at the top of the tomato to make a lid, but do not cut all the way. Remove pulp and turn tomato shells upside down to drain. Remove seeds from pulp and chop the pulp. Continue as directed in the recipe.

Steamed Matchstick Carrots and Celery

1 pound carrots, cut into very thin strips

1 pound celery, cut into similar matchstick pieces

1 tablespoon butter

2 teaspoons dried thyme

¼ teaspoon salt

In a large skillet, sprinkle the vegetables with 3 tablespoons water. Add the butter, cut into small pieces; sprinkle with salt. Cover the vegetables with wax paper and a lid. Cook for about 15 minutes until fork-tender.

6–8 portions

Eggplant and Zucchini Stuffed with Rice and Tomatoes

4 small eggplants

⅓ cup olive oil

4 small zucchini

10 ounces frozen spinach

2 ounces cherry tomatoes

2 medium-size onions, chopped

2 cloves garlic, minced

¾ cup rice, precooked

3 tablespoons mixed fresh herbs (parsley, marjoram, chives), minced

½ teaspoon salt, freshly ground pepper

½ cup parmesan cheese, freshly grated

1. Preheat oven to 400°.
2. Cut the eggplants in half lengthwise and score. Leaving the flesh intact, use a grapefruit knife to cut around the edge of the eggplant to leave a ¼″ wall. Put face down in a pan that has been drizzled with 2 tablespoons olive oil. Bake at 400° for about 10 minutes or until flesh is slightly soft and browned.
3. Cut the zucchini in the same fashion as the eggplant and brown in 2 tablespoons olive oil in the oven for about 13 minutes.
4. Scoop out the pulp of both vegetables with a melon baller and chop. Set aside.
5. Cook the frozen spinach in boiling water about 4–5 minutes until it separates. Refresh under cold water and drain. Gather the spinach in small amounts and squeeze by the handful until dry. Chop and set aside.
6. Cut cherry tomatoes in half, scrape seeds from the pulp, and chop.
7. Cook the onions with the garlic in 1 tablespoon olive oil for about 5 minutes over medium heat until they are translucent but not browned. Add the eggplant and zucchini and continue to cook for 5–10 minutes.
8. Mix the spinach, tomato pulp, rice, herbs, salt, and pepper with the onion-eggplant-zucchini mixture and divide among the vegetable shells. Sprinkle parmesan cheese over the fillings and top with a drop of olive oil.
9. Bake at 400° for 10 minutes or until slightly brown.

8 portions of each vegetable

Monkey Bread

½ ounce dry yeast

½ cup lukewarm water

1 cup milk

⅔ cup sugar

⅔ cup shortening

2 teaspoons salt

1 cup mashed potatoes
  (or reconstituted instant)

2 eggs

5–6 cups flour

2 tablespoons butter, melted

1. Dissolve the yeast in the lukewarm water and let proof.
2. Scald the milk and add sugar and shortening to the hot liquid (it is not necessary for the shortening to melt completely). Mix all the ingredients together and let rise for 2 hours.
3. Punch down, cover, and place in refrigerator until cold or overnight.
4. Preheat oven to 350°.
5. Knead about 10 minutes on a lightly floured surface until the dough is elastic and pliable. Pinch off small amounts of the dough and shape into balls the size of a walnut. Dip in melted butter and fill a large Bundt pan ⅔ full. Let rise 2 hours.
6. Bake at 350° for 35 minutes.

12 – 16 portions

Baked Vidalia Onion

A perfect accompaniment for roasted or grilled meats, the Vidalia onion has practically no calories and a wonderful sweet flavor when baked.

Cut the top from a Vidalia onion and sprinkle with salt, freshly ground pepper, and minced fresh herbs (tarragon, chives, parsley or summer savory, and thyme). Top with a pat of butter and wrap in aluminum foil. Bake at 375° for 35–40 minutes or until tender.

For a quicker version of chocolate curls, pull a vegetable peeler across the surface of a piece of good-quality chocolate.

Poached Pears with Raspberry Sauce and Chocolate Curls

6 pears

1 bottle (750 ml) red wine

2 cups water

½ cup sugar

½ teaspoon vanilla

1 teaspoon cloves

1 10-ounce package frozen raspberries

¼–½ cup sugar

1 tablespoon Grand Marnier

4 ounces semisweet chocolate

½ pint heavy cream, whipped

1. Select pears that are firm but not hard. Peel leaving the stem intact.
2. Combine wine, water, ½ cup sugar, vanilla, and cloves in a medium saucepan and bring to a boil. Poach the pears in barely simmering liquid for about 20 minutes until they are tender and pink in color. Remove pears from pan and set aside.
3. Thaw the raspberries and put through a strainer to remove seeds. Add ¼–½ cup sugar and Grand Marnier.
4. Melt the chocolate over low heat and smear in a thick layer on a marble slab with a spatula. As it begins to harden and lose its shine, pull a pastry scraper or spatula across the surface to make curls.
5. To serve, divide the raspberry sauce among 6 dessert plates and set the pears upright on top of the sauce. Decorate with shaved chocolate. Garnish with lemon balm or mint, or put browned slivered almonds on top if desired. Pass sweetened whipped cream separately.

6 portions

Dessert
after the Symphony
in the Little House

(An All-Chocolate Evening)

Chocolate Cheesecake with Raspberry Sauce

Fresh Strawberries Dipped in Chocolate

Chocolate-Covered Roasted Pecans

Chocolate Roulade with Coffee Ice Cream and
Kahlua Sauce

Candied Orange and Grapefruit Peel Dipped
in Chocolate

Amaretto Truffles

*   *   *

Champagne

Serves 8–10 people

The Little House, located just behind Fearrington House, was once used as the office for the farm. Those who had farm business to conduct presented themselves at its door instead of taking muddy feet inside the main farmhouse.

Today it has been refurbished and is used for private dining.

Chocolate Cheesecake with Raspberry Sauce

Crust

3 cups graham cracker crumbs

2 ounces semisweet chocolate

1½ sticks butter, melted

3 tablespoons sugar

Filling

3 eggs

1 cup sugar

3 8-ounce packages cream cheese, softened

12 ounces semisweet chocolate

1½ sticks butter

1 cup sour cream

1 teaspoon vanilla

1 cup pecans, coarsely chopped

1 recipe Raspberry Sauce

1. Preheat oven to 325°.
2. To make the graham cracker crust, pulverize the crackers in a food processor with quick on and off turns. Grate 2 ounces chocolate in the same work bowl and combine with the crumbs, melted butter, and 3 tablespoons sugar. Press the mixture into two 8½″ springform pans, spreading it evenly on the bottom and partially up the sides. Set aside.
3. To make the filling, beat the eggs with the sugar until the mixture is thick and ribbons when the beater is lifted. Add the softened cream cheese and whip until the mixture is smooth.
4. Melt the chocolate with the butter by setting in a saucepan over the lowest possible flame on a gas stove (otherwise use a double boiler). Add the sour cream and vanilla and blend with the cream cheese–egg mixture.
5. Divide the cheesecake mixture between the 2 crusts and bake at 325° for 2 hours. Let the cakes cool, remove them from the springform pans, and chill for several hours.
6. To serve, slice one cheesecake (freeze the other) and nap with 2–3 tablespoons of the raspberry sauce. Garnish with fresh raspberries, if available.

Yields two 8½″ cheesecakes, each serving 8–10 people

This cheesecake has been a favorite in our household for almost 20 years. It freezes beautifully and can be thawed quickly if one has a middle-of-the-night craving for chocolate. Its versatility is superb. Decorate it with holly at Christmas and serve it with a cranberry-raspberry sauce.

For St. Valentine's Day it can be served with a strawberry sauce and fresh strawberries. Use glazed cherries over the top for Washington's Birthday. Garnish with fresh violets and leaves in the spring, or serve with Grand Marnier sauce and poached pieces of orange peel (long and thin) for a treat that's delicious any time of the year.

Raspberry Sauce

2 10-ounce packages frozen raspberries

¼–½ cup sugar

2 tablespoons raspberry liqueur (Framboise) or Grand Marnier

Bring the raspberries to room temperature and push the pulp through a drum sieve or strainer with a large spoon to remove the seeds. Season to taste with sugar and liqueur.

The sauce may be kept in the refrigerator for several weeks.

Yields approximately 1 cup

Kahlua Sauce

1 tablespoon unsalted
  butter
5 ounces half-and-half
1 cup sugar
4 ounces unsweetened
  chocolate
1½ tablespoons
  Kahlua

Melt the butter with the
half-and-half and sugar, stirring until the mixture is
opaque and the sugar is dissolved. Add the chocolate and
whisk until the chocolate
melts. Remove from the
stove, cool slightly, and add
Kahlua.
  Variation: Add 2 table-
spoons of Grand Marnier,
rum, or Framboise for extra
flavor.

Yields 1¼ cups

Lisa Dilts

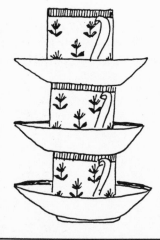

Chocolate Roulade with Coffee Ice Cream and Kahlua Sauce

5 eggs

1 cup confectioners' sugar

½ teaspoon vanilla

4 tablespoons cocoa

2 tablespoons confectioners' sugar

1 recipe Coffee Ice Cream

1 recipe Kahlua Sauce

½ cup slivered almonds, lightly browned

optional: 1 recipe Chocolate Leaves for garnish

1. Preheat oven to 325°.
2. Separate the eggs and beat the yolks, adding the cup of sugar gradually until thick and creamy. Add the vanilla.
3. Beat the egg whites until they hold soft peaks. Continue to beat and add the cocoa 1 tablespoon at a time. Fold lightly into the yolk mixture and spread into a 15″ × 10½″ jelly roll pan that has been lined with parchment paper and greased.
4. Bake at 325° for 20–25 minutes or until the cake shrinks from the edges of the pan. With the paper side up, turn out onto a clean cloth that has been dusted with 2 tablespoons confectioners' sugar. Peel off the paper and cover the cake with a slightly dampened cloth. Cool.
5. Spread half the coffee ice cream onto the cake; freeze the rest for another time. Begin forming the roulade by using the cloth underneath to aid in rolling evenly into a log shape. Place the roll on a cookie sheet with the seam side down and freeze until serving time.
6. To serve, nap the bottom of a dessert plate with Kahlua sauce and top it with a slice of the roulade. Garnish with browned almonds. For a more elegant presentation, garnish each plate with chocolate leaves.

6–8 portions

Coffee Ice Cream

2 cups milk

1 cup sugar

¼ teaspoon salt

2 eggs, lightly beaten

1 teaspoon vanilla

3 tablespoons rum

1 cup heavy cream

½ cup strong coffee

½ teaspoon nutmeg,
  freshly grated

1. Scald the milk. Cool slightly.
2. Mix the sugar and salt with the eggs. Pour about half the hot milk into the egg-sugar mixture, stirring constantly. Slowly pour the egg-sugar mixture back into the saucepan. Cook 15–20 minutes over low heat, stirring constantly until it has thickened and coats the back of a spoon. Cool. Blend in the vanilla and the rum.
3. Combine the custard mixture with heavy cream, coffee, and nutmeg. Freeze in an ice cream maker.

8–10 portions

Autumn Flower Arrangement
Fresh and Dried Flowers

One attractive fall arrangement uses only six fresh flowers. All the rest are dried. There are two types of statice (blue and white), wheat, empress tree pods, and six large chrysanthemums.

The colors are definitely fall. Everything is tan-bronze except for the blue statice.

Empress tree pods,
chrysanthemums,
statice

Chocolate Leaves*

These decorative garnishes can be kept indefinitely in the refrigerator.

6 ounces semisweet chocolate

1 ounce butter

2 tablespoons light corn syrup

⅛ bar paraffin

18 rose, violet, or other heavily veined leaves

vegetable oil

1. Using the very lowest possible flame on a gas stove (or in the top of a double boiler), melt the chocolate, butter, corn syrup, and paraffin, stirring occasionally until smooth.
2. Wash the leaves, pat them dry, and brush them with vegetable oil. While the chocolate is still warm spread the mixture on the *back* of each leaf to a thickness of no more than ⅛". Be careful not to let the chocolate dribble on the back side of the leaf, since that makes peeling more difficult.
3. Refrigerate until firm. When ready to use, peel the green leaf away and discard it.

Yields 18 leaves

* Extra Recipe

Candied Orange and Grapefruit Peel Dipped in Chocolate

Grapefruit Peel

1. Cut each grapefruit in half and then each half in four pieces. Remove all the fruit and its membranes, but leave the white pith in place at this time. Collect the rinds and store in refrigerator for 3–4 days in sealed plastic bags.
2. Soak peel overnight in a large container, covering it with water mixed with 1 tablespoon salt.
3. Drain, cover again with cold water, and bring to boiling point. Cook for 15–20 minutes. Drain and repeat the procedure 3 more times. Drain and cool. With a sharp knife scrape the white pith from the peel. Cut peel in strips about ⅜" wide.
4. For each cup of peel, make a syrup consisting of 1 cup sugar and ½ cup water. Bring to a boil, add the strips of peel, and simmer for about 20 minutes until the peel is translucent and much of the syrup is absorbed. Remove with a slotted spoon and cool on a cake rack.
5. Roll strips in granulated sugar and set out to dry on the cake rack for a few hours. (This last step is important: especially if the peel is to be stored in a tin for several weeks, it must not be too soft.)

Orange Peel

The procedure is the same as for grapefruit peel through the overnight soaking, but not as time-consuming later.

1. Follow steps 1 and 2 of the grapefruit peel recipe above.
2. Drain, cover with cold water, and cook for 30 minutes. Drain, remove white pith, and cut into strips. Boil in the sugar syrup until the peel is translucent and has absorbed most of the syrup.
3. Remove peel with a slotted spoon and set it out to cool on a cake rack. Roll in granulated sugar and let dry for a few hours.
4. Dip one edge in melted chocolate and cool on a cake rack.

Amaretto Truffles

34 ounces semisweet chocolate

¾ cup heavy cream, heated in a heavy-bottomed saucepan

2 teaspoons butter, room temperature

½ teaspoon almond extract

2 tablespoons amaretto liqueur

1 egg yolk, room temperature

6 ounces Amaretti di Saronno cookies, crushed

1. Chop 10 ounces chocolate in small pieces and add to warm heavy cream. Melt, stirring over low heat. Remove from heat and add butter, almond extract, and amaretto. Stir in egg yolk and transfer mixture to a small bowl. Cover and freeze for several hours.

2. To make the centers, scoop out filling into 1″ balls with a melon baller. Dust melon baller and your hands lightly with confectioners' sugar if needed. Cover the centers and freeze them for 1 hour.

3. Finely chop 4 ounces chocolate and set aside. Melt the remaining chocolate in a double boiler, remove from heat, and add the chopped chocolate to the mixture, stirring to melt.

4. Remove the centers from the freezer. Working quickly, dip each center in melted chocolate and place on a parchment-lined sheet. Top each truffle with a pinch of Amaretti di Saronno cookie crumbs.

5. Set chocolate by chilling truffles uncovered in the refrigerator for 30 minutes. Store in an airtight refrigerated tin.

Yields approximately 3 dozen truffles

Karen Barker

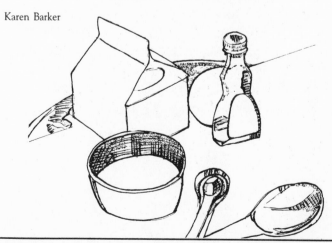

Thanksgiving Day

Carrot Soup with Bacon and Orange Peel

*   *   *

Roast Turkey with Apricot Walnut Dressing

Smithfield Ham

Corn Soufflé with Sweet Golden Peppers

Baked Acorn Squash with Spinach and Pine Nuts

French Green Beans

Pickled Beets

*   *   *

Fresh Pumpkin Pie with Ginger Whipped Cream

Persimmon Chiffon Pie

Serves 6–8 people

Corn, chrysanthemums, goldenrod

Carrot Soup with Bacon and Orange Peel

2 tablespoons butter

3 leeks, rinsed, cleaned, drained, and chopped

6 cups chicken stock

2 cups water

1 turnip, peeled and diced

1 potato, peeled and diced

10 carrots, peeled and diced

½ teaspoon salt, freshly ground pepper

1 pint heavy cream

½ cup sour cream

4 ounces bacon, fried, drained, and chopped

2 orange rinds, cut into ¼"
wide matchsticks and poached

1. Melt the butter and cook the leeks over medium heat for 8–10 minutes until they are translucent but not browned.
2. Add the chicken stock, water, turnip, potato, carrots, salt, and pepper and bring to a boil. Simmer about 20 minutes until the potato and turnip are tender.
3. Cool slightly and purée in a blender or food processor. Blend in heavy cream. Heat through.
4. To serve, garnish each bowl with 1 tablespoon sour cream, bacon, and orange rind.

6–8 portions

To add the lightest touch of sweetness to the orange rind, poach it in 2 cups water and ½ cup sugar for 3 minutes.

To add color to the soup, replace the bacon with thinly sliced scallions.

Autumn Flower Arrangement

The farmer down the road leaves us a small patch of corn each year when he harvests the field. By this time it has dried in the field naturally and is bleached to a shade of tan.

Corn
Chrysanthemum
Goldenrod

A large can is filled with soaked oasis and water to accommodate the flowers.

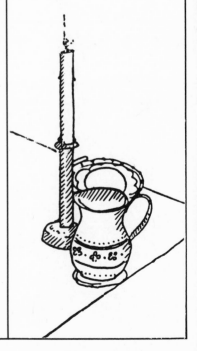

Country Ham

Clean the ham by scraping off the mold and pepper. Wash well with soap and hot water, using a brush. Rinse. Put the ham in a large stockpot skin side down and cover it with cold water. Bring to a boil and simmer for 20–25 minutes per pound. Let the ham cool in the cooking water; then remove it from the pan and take off the skin. It may be put in the oven to brown at this point, but browning is not necessary.

Apricot Walnut Dressing

Baked dressing is a tradition in the South as an accompaniment to turkey. This recipe has a delightful flavor and is quite a departure from the usual "plain bread" or seafood stuffings.

1 cup dried apricots

2 tablespoons unbleached flour

¾ cup golden raisins

2 tablespoons bourbon or dark rum

2 cups walnut pieces

2 medium-size garlic cloves

2 medium-size onions

4 medium-size celery ribs

1½ sticks butter

12 cups fresh white bread crumbs
   (prefer thin-sliced Pepperidge Farm)

½ teaspoon salt, freshly ground black pepper

1 cup chicken stock

2 tablespoons sage

1. Preheat oven to 350°.
2. Chop apricots coarsely by using quick on and off turns of the processor. Stir in flour, raisins, and bourbon or rum. Set aside at room temperature for 1 hour.
3. Chop walnuts coarsely and add to apricot mixture.
4. If using a food processor, drop garlic cloves down the feed tube to mince finely; add onions and celery and finely chop. Sauté 3–4 minutes in 4 tablespoons butter and add to apricot mixture.
5. Melt the remaining butter and mix well with bread crumbs, salt, pepper, chicken stock, and sage. Blend with apricot mixture. Spread into a 13″ × 9½″ baking dish and bake 20 minutes at 350°.

8–10 portions

Walter Royal

Corn Soufflé with Sweet Golden Peppers

3 tablespoons butter, softened

4 tablespoons parmesan cheese, freshly grated

1 small onion, finely minced

½ yellow bell pepper, finely minced

3 tablespoons flour

¼ teaspoon salt, freshly ground white pepper

¼ teaspoon paprika

½ teaspoon dry mustard

¾ cup hot milk

few drops Tabasco

6 eggs

2 cups fresh corn (6–8 ears)

¼ teaspoon cream of tartar, pinch of salt

½ cup white cheddar cheese, grated

1. Preheat oven to 350°.
2. Grease a 2-quart soufflé dish with 1½ teaspoons butter, and sprinkle the sides and bottom with 2 tablespoons parmesan cheese. Set aside.
3. Melt 2½ tablespoons butter in a large saucepan. Cook the onion and pepper over medium heat for about 5 minutes. Mix the flour with the salt, pepper, paprika, and dry mustard. Blend into the mixture and cook for 2 minutes, being careful not to brown the mixture.
4. Remove from heat and beat in the hot milk all at once, stirring vigorously with a whisk. Return to the stove and boil for 1 minute, stirring constantly. Add Tabasco.
5. Separate the 6 eggs (reserving the whites for later use) and beat 3 yolks into the hot sauce. The base may be prepared ahead of time to this point.
6. Cut the corn kernels from the ears and scrape the cob to get the milky substance. Add both to the base.
7. Beat the 6 egg whites until they begin to foam. Add a pinch of salt and the cream of tartar and continue beating until the whites form stiff peaks.
8. Stir ⅓ of the beaten egg whites into the hot mixture to lighten it. Add the cheddar, the remaining parmesan, and the rest of the beaten egg whites. Fold the mixtures together quickly with a rubber spatula, turning the bowl and mixing from the center out to the edges of the pan.
9. Fill the prepared soufflé dish ⅔ full and set the dish in the center of a larger baking dish that has been filled with hot water. The water should come halfway up the sides of the soufflé dish. Bake at 350° for 1¼ hours. The soufflé is done when it has risen 2″ above the rim of the soufflé dish.

6–8 portions

The soufflé can be un-molded. Run a knife around its outside edge. Turn a lightly buttered round serving platter upside down over the top of the soufflé dish. Hold both the dishes as a unit and flip the platter right side up with a sharp jerk; the soufflé should drop. Surround it with blanched vegetables.

Grated Sweet Potato Pudding*

2 eggs

¼ cup sugar

¼ teaspoon salt

¼ cup maple syrup

1 cup milk

3 cups raw sweet potatoes, grated

2 tablespoons butter, melted

1 teaspoon nutmeg

½ cup pecans, chopped

1. Preheat oven to 375°.
2. Beat the eggs well and add the sugar, salt, syrup, and milk.
3. Blend the potatoes, butter, nutmeg, and pecans with the egg mixture and pour into a buttered 11¾" × 7½" pan.
4. Bake for 50–60 minutes at 375°.

6–8 portions

* Extra Recipe

Baked Acorn Squash with Spinach and Pine Nuts

3–4 acorn squash, 3½" in diameter

4 tablespoons butter

½ teaspoon salt, freshly ground pepper

freshly grated nutmeg

3 tablespoons pine nuts

3 pounds fresh spinach

1. Preheat oven to 375°.
2. Cut the squash in half and remove the seeds. Melt 1 tablespoon butter and brush all cut surfaces. Season with ¼ teaspoon salt, pepper, and nutmeg. Cover with foil and bake (cut side up) for 35 minutes at 375° until the flesh is tender when pierced with a fork. Remove from the oven and set aside.
3. Sauté the pine nuts in a small skillet in 1 tablespoon butter until they are golden. Set aside to drain on absorbent towels.
4. Wash the spinach to remove any possible grit. Remove the coarse main stem. Cook the spinach in a skillet over medium high heat in the water that clings to the leaves after washing. When the spinach wilts, add the remaining butter and salt, pepper, nutmeg, and pine nuts. Heat through, spoon mixture into squash, and serve.

6–8 portions

Cabbages
on the table

Autumn Flower Arrangement
Cabbages on the Table

This arrangement is a Thanksgiving Day tradition at Fearrington House and can always be found on the mirrored table for the holidays.

Components of the arrangement are:

Cabbage
Flowering cabbage
Flowering kale
Purple chrysanthemums
Deodora cedar branches

Line the table with plastic and cedar branches. Begin putting cabbages in place, folding the outer leaves backwards for a fuller, more open look.

Wash the ornamental cabbages and kale to rid them of any insects, and cut off the stems. Arrange on the table, distributing the purple and white colors evenly.

Fill water vials and insert cut stems of chrysanthemums. Tuck among the rolled leaves of the cabbages.

French Green Beans

This is a recipe my mother has done for many years. Its preparation is so simple that one would not expect such wonderful results.

1 pound green beans

½ teaspoon salt

3 pieces bacon

¼ cup green or red bell pepper, minced

1 small onion, minced

1. Wash and string the beans, and cut them in half lengthwise.
2. In a large pot place 2″ of water with salt and bring to a boil. Add the beans and simmer covered for 30 minutes.
3. Fry the bacon until crisp and set aside to drain. Remove all but 1 tablespoon of fat from the pan. Sauté the green pepper and onion in the remaining fat. Cook about 10 minutes until tender.
4. Drain the liquid from the beans. Add the onion and bell pepper mixture to the pot. Blend well so that the seasonings thoroughly mix with the beans. To serve, garnish with chopped bacon.

6–8 portions

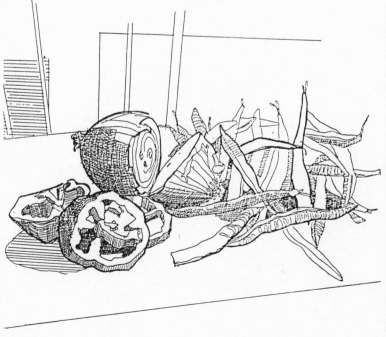

Brussels Sprouts and Leeks*

1½ pounds brussels sprouts

3 tablespoons butter

1 small red bell pepper, finely chopped

4–5 leeks, washed and sliced

2 cloves garlic, minced

½ teaspoon salt, freshly ground white pepper

⅓ cup parmesan cheese, freshly grated

¼ cup pine nuts, toasted

1. Trim, wash, and drain brussels sprouts. Cook in boiling water about 8 minutes until tender but still firm when pierced with a fork. Refresh under cold water, drain, and set aside.
2. Melt the butter in a skillet. Add the bell pepper, leeks, celery, garlic, salt, and pepper, and cook over moderate heat for about 10 minutes. Cut the brussels sprouts in half and add to the pan to heat through.
3. Blend in parmesan cheese, sprinkle with pine nuts, and serve.

6–8 portions

Joaquin Fowler

* Extra Recipe

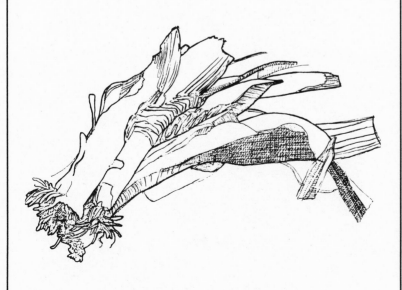

Pickled Beets

1½ pounds fresh beets
½ cup water
½ cup cider vinegar
½ cup sugar
2 cloves
*½ teaspoon pickling
    spices, tied in
    cheesecloth*

1. *Cut the tops from the beets, leaving 1" of the stem intact, and wash. Bring water to a boil and cook the beets for 30–45 minutes (depending on the size) until tender when pierced by a fork. Drain, reserving the juice, and cool. Slip the skins and cut the beets into wedges.*
2. *Combine the water, vinegar, sugar, and cloves and bring to a boil. Add pickling spices and stir until sugar dissolves. Pour over the beets. Serve at room temperature.*

6 portions

The beets are boiled with part of the stem intact to keep them from bleeding. Otherwise the red color would be partially drained from the vegetable.

Cabbage with Bacon and Croutons*

2 pounds cabbage

4 slices bacon

2 slices white bread

1½ tablespoons butter

1 teaspoon salt, freshly ground pepper

4 scallions, chopped

2 tablespoons chives, minced

optional: 1 sun-dried tomato packed in oil, patted dry, and minced

1. Shred the cabbage by stacking the leaves, holding them tightly, and cutting with a knife. Place in a colander, rinse, and drain.
2. Fry the bacon until crisp and set on absorbent towels to drain, leaving the fat in the pan.
3. Remove the bread crusts and cut the bread into cubes. Melt 1½ tablespoons butter in a skillet and brown the cubes over medium heat.
4. Place the cabbage in the bacon pan, using only the water that clings to the leaves from washing. Incorporate bacon fat with cabbage as it cooks over medium heat for about 5 minutes or until the water evaporates and the cabbage is limp. Toss with salt, pepper, croutons, scallions, chives, and bits of the sun-dried tomato.

6 portions

* Extra Recipe

Fresh Pumpkin Pie with Ginger Whipped Cream

1 unbaked 9″ pie shell
(recipe p. 100)

6 pastry turkeys

3 eggs

1¾ cups milk

⅔ cup brown sugar (packed)

2 tablespoons white sugar

¼ teaspoon salt

1¾ cups fresh pumpkin,
cooked and drained

1¼ teaspoons cinnamon

½ teaspoon ground ginger

½ teaspoon nutmeg,
freshly grated

½ teaspoon ground cloves

1 teaspoon vanilla or
2 tablespoons brandy or rum

1 cup pecans, chopped

1 recipe Ginger Whipped Cream

1. Preheat oven to 425°. Make pie shell. Cut pastry turkeys from pastry scraps with a cookie cutter and bake until golden.
2. Beat eggs and add milk, sugars, salt, and pumpkin.
3. Blend the spices and vanilla with the pumpkin mixture and pour into unbaked pie shell. Sprinkle chopped nuts around outside edge.
4. Bake at 425° for 45–55 minutes.
5. Serve warm or cool with ginger whipped cream and pastry turkeys.

6–8 portions

Ginger Whipped Cream

1 cup heavy cream

1½ teaspoons dark rum

¼ teaspoon ground ginger

2 tablespoons sugar

1. In the bowl of an electric mixer, whip the cream until it becomes thickened.
2. Add rum, ginger, and sugar gradually, continuing to beat until the mixture holds soft peaks.

There are two ways of preparing the pumpkin pulp. Both begin with washing the pumpkin, cutting it in half, and removing the seeds and strings.

In the first method, bake the two halves at 325° for about 1 hour or until tender. Remove the pulp from the shell and purée in a food processor.

In the second method, cut the pumpkin into large chunks and remove rind. Place the pulp in a large container with a small amount of water and bring to a boil. Simmer until tender. Drain for a long time in a colander, pressing often to remove all excess water.

Whereas the American persimmon (Diospyros virginiana) *should be used in the pie because it is tastier, the Japanese persimmon* (Diospyros kaki) *makes a better garnish because it is prettier.*

Persimmon Chiffon Pie

1 prebaked 9″ pie shell (recipe p. 100)

1 cup persimmon pulp

½ teaspoon vanilla

4 egg yolks, beaten

1 teaspoon lemon juice

½ teaspoon salt

½ cup sugar

1 tablespoon gelatin

½ cup water

4 egg whites

2 tablespoons sugar

1 pint heavy cream, whipped

1. Peel the persimmons, cut in half, and remove the seeds. Purée in a food processor with the vanilla to make 1 cup pulp.
2. Cook the egg yolks, lemon juice, salt, and ½ cup sugar in the top of a double boiler until thickened, stirring occasionally. Combine with the puréed persimmons.
3. Soften the gelatin in water and add to the persimmon pulp and yolk mixture, stirring until gelatin is dissolved. Chill.
4. Beat the egg whites until they hold soft peaks. Gradually add 2 tablespoons sugar and continue beating until the mixture holds stiff peaks. Fold into the chilled pulp and yolk mixture. Spread the filling into the prebaked pie shell, and top with whipped cream. Chill. Garnish with bright orange slices of Japanese persimmon.

6–8 portions

Mary Ryon

Tea in the Afternoon

Black Walnut Chocolate Pound Cake

Heart-Shaped Scones with Currants

Miniature Glazed Orange Muffins

Almond Crescent Cookies

Roasted Pecans

Pecan Date Cheese Straws

Lemon Curd Tartlettes with Candied Violets

Cucumber Sandwiches

Serves 10–12 people

Fall-blooming cyclamen

Black Walnut Chocolate Pound Cake

1 cup butter (2 sticks)	2¾ cups flour
½ cup shortening	¾ cup cocoa
3 cups sugar	½ teaspoon baking powder
5 eggs	¼ teaspoon salt
2 tablespoons rum	1 cup milk
½ teaspoon vanilla	1½ cups black walnuts, chopped

1. Preheat oven to 325°.
2. Cream butter and shortening with sugar until light and fluffy. Add eggs one at a time, rum, and vanilla.
3. Remove 2 tablespoons flour from the measured amount before sifting and toss the chopped walnuts in it.
4. Sift the flour, cocoa, baking powder, and salt together. Add to the egg mixture alternately with the milk, beginning and ending with the dry ingredients. Fold in floured chopped nuts.
5. Grease one 9″ tube pan and line the bottom with wax paper. Grease the paper and flour it. Pour batter into the pan and bake at 325° for 1¼ hours or until a toothpick inserted into the middle of the cake comes out clean. Let cool in the pan before removing.

Yields 20 portions or 1 tube cake

Autumn Flower Arrangement
Fall-Blooming Cyclamen

Dig the cyclamen from the garden just as it begins to bloom (it has no leaves at this stage of its development), and put it in a shallow pot with dirt.

Line the basket with heavy plastic and set items in place.

The components used are:

Violets (with dirt)
Ferns (with dirt)
Moss from the woods (2 kinds)
Mushrooms from the woods
Pipsissewas (with dirt)
Bark with lichen
Pinecones

The arrangement will last for several weeks if properly cared for. Water lightly once a week and mist occasionally.

Heart-Shaped Scones with Currants

½ cup currants

2 cups unbleached flour

1¾ teaspoons baking powder

1 tablespoon sugar

¼ teaspoon salt

½ cup butter

1 cup cream

1 egg yolk

1 tablespoon water

2 tablespoons sugar

For the very best variation on this recipe, in place of the currants use ½ cup golden raisins (not plumped) and add the minced rind of 1 orange to the dough.

Serve with butter and three-fruit marmalade.

1. Preheat oven to 400°.
2. Plump the currants in ¼ cup warm water.
3. Sift the flour, baking powder, 1 tablespoon sugar, and salt together. Blend in butter with a pastry cutter until the mixture is the size of small peas. Incorporate the cream and currants, handling the dough as little as possible.
4. Gather the dough together and roll it out on a lightly floured board until it is ½"–¾" thick. Cut into heart shapes with a 2" long heart-shaped cookie cutter.
5. Brush with egg yolk and water mixture as a glaze, sprinkle with sugar, and bake at 400° for about 15 minutes until golden.

Yields 2 dozen scones

Miniature Glazed Orange Muffins

1 egg

¾ cup buttermilk

1 orange rind, grated

¼ cup orange juice

4 ounces butter, melted

1¾ cups unbleached flour

⅓ cup sugar

1 teaspoon baking powder

½ teaspoon salt

½ teaspoon baking soda

1 recipe Orange Glaze

1. Preheat oven to 400°.
2. Beat egg lightly. Stir in buttermilk, orange rind, orange juice, and melted butter. Sift dry ingredients together, add to the liquid ingredients, and stir until just mixed. The batter should be lumpy; do not overmix.
3. Fill greased muffin cups (or use muffin liners) ⅔ full. Bake 20–25 minutes at 400°. Prepare glaze while muffins are baking.
4. Remove muffins from oven. Run knife around edges of muffin cups. While the muffins are still warm, prick the tops lightly and pour glaze over. Remove from pan when cool.

Yields 2 dozen muffins

Orange Glaze

¾ cup sugar

¾ cup orange juice

1 teaspoon lemon juice

1 orange rind, grated

Combine all ingredients; cook and stir until the sugar is dissolved. The mixture should come to a soft simmer and make a light syrup.

Two recipes for this menu appear in other parts of the book. Cucumber Sandwiches are on p. 54. For the Lemon Curd Tartlettes, use the All-Purpose Pastry recipe on p. 53 for tart shells and the Lemon Curd recipe on p. 104 for filling; garnish with fresh or candied violets.

Almond Crescent Cookies

1 cup butter

1 cup sugar

2 cups flour

1 cup almonds, ground in food processor

1 teaspoon vanilla

2 teaspoons orange or lemon rind, grated

confectioners' sugar

1. Preheat oven to 300°.
2. Cream butter and sugar. Mix with flour, almonds, vanilla, and grated rind.
3. Break off small pieces of dough, shape into 2″ pencil strips, and arrange on a cookie sheet, turning ends toward each other to form a crescent.
4. Bake at 300° for 35 minutes. Cool. Roll in confectioners' sugar.

Yields approximately 4 dozen cookies

Pecan Date Cheese Straws

1 pound sharp cheddar cheese, grated

2 cups flour

½ teaspoon salt

¼ teaspoon cayenne pepper

1 stick butter, softened

5 dozen dates

5 dozen whole pecan halves

1. Preheat oven to 400°.
2. Mix cheese with flour, salt, cayenne, and butter. Stuff each date with a pecan half and cover with the cheese straw dough by rolling and shaping the pieces by hand.
3. Place on an ungreased cookie sheet and bake for 10 minutes at 400°.

Yields 5 dozen cheese straws

Autumn Projects

1. Herb Wreath

2. Bouquet Garni

3. Potpourri

Herb wreath

Herb Wreath

The following materials are needed for an herb wreath:

Straw wreath   **Grosgrain ribbon**

Florist pins   **Culinary or fragrance herbs**

The following are optional:

Cinnamon sticks   **Whole nutmegs**

Dried orange peel   **Cloves**

Start by covering the wreath uniformly with Southern wormwood, making certain that the plant material is facing the same direction. Pin the wormwood on the front face of the wreath in such a manner that it extends over both the inside and outside edges of the form. Its silver-gray foliage is very versatile and can serve as a base for either a culinary wreath or a fragrance wreath.

Lamb's ear may be pinned in place fresh. It dries naturally and will give an interesting texture to the wreath.

Arrange and pin combinations of herbs (such as oregano, dill flowerheads, thyme, rosemary, and sage) in clusters. Finish with a grosgrain ribbon bow pinned in place as the last decoration.

If the wreath is to be given as a gift, tie a small pair of scissors to the base and stick the points into the base, thus allowing the new owner to actually cut and use the dried herbs.

A *culinary wreath* could contain thyme, oregano, rosemary, bay leaves, sage, chive flowers, and summer savory. Almost any combination of herbs will work, but the point is to use herbs grown in the summer garden. Among other additions to the culinary wreath, cinnamon sticks can be pushed directly into the straw base. Orange peel can be removed from the fruit in spirals, left to air-dry for three days, and pinned in place for a splash of color. Drill holes in nutmegs and use wire to secure them to the wreath. Push a few cloves around the edges for spicy fragrance.

Harvesting the herbs for a *fragrance wreath* does not take place until the fall. They may be enjoyed in the summer garden for texture and fragrance and then snatched just before frost. Pineapple sage may be tied in bunches and hung upside down or dried on screens. Lemon verbena foliage keeps its bright green color even after it has dried; its leaves should be stripped from the stem and dried on screens for two or three days. The flat but textured leaves of scented geraniums offer limitless possibilities, since there are so many varieties. The lemon geranium has curly leaves and a clean, lemony smell; some will remember that this was the herb placed in fingerbowls at fancy Victorian restaurants. Other additions could be lemon balm, lemon thyme, the whole family of mints (including orange mint, spearmint, and peppermint), cloves, and dried lemon and orange peel.

Bouquet Garni

Growing one's own herbs and being able to use them fresh is a real pleasure. To dry them for a bouquet garni is another reward from the summer garden. (See pp. 129–31 for instructions for drying individual herbs.)

A bouquet garni consists of blended herbs tied together in a cheesecloth pouch and is used to flavor soups, stews, or sauces. Any combination of herbs may be used, but a traditional recipe always includes parsley, thyme, and bay leaf. An all-purpose bouquet garni might include additions of oregano, lemon thyme, sage, and winter savory.

Strip the previously dried leaves from the branches and clean any debris. Cut a circle 3″ in diameter from good-quality cheesecloth. Mix the herbs, using 1 bay leaf and 1-teaspoon amounts of the others, plus a dash of celery seed. Place the herbs in the center of the cheesecloth and make a pouch by pulling the cloth around the herbs and tying it tightly with thread.

For a bouquet garni for fish, use dried marjoram (it is said to be sweeter than oregano), lemon balm, lemon thyme, parsley, a bay leaf, and a few whole white peppercorns.

Potpourri

This potpourri, with its pine oil, has the smells of Christmas. It is made with dried herbs in the fall, left for the scents to develop, and divided into packets just in time for Christmas.

1 cup lemon verbena, dried	8 ounces whole allspice
2 quarts rose petals, dried	8 ounces whole nutmegs
1 cup marigold petals, dried	6 ounces pineapple sage
1½ cups cedar chips	16 ounces rosemary leaves, dried
8 ounces cinnamon pieces	4 ounces orris root
8 ounces whole cloves	1½ ounces pine oil

Some optional elements are:

pinecones

orange peel, dried

scented geraniums

mint and orange mint, dried

Mix together all the herbs and flowers in a large tub. Be certain that all ingredients have been dried and that no moisture remains on the leaves.

In a separate bowl combine the orris root and pine oil, being certain no lumps remain. Mix thoroughly with the flowers and herbs. Cover as tightly as possible and set aside for at least 4 weeks to let the flavors ripen.

These amounts yield about 1½ gallons of potpourri.

Four-ounce packets of potpourri placed inside decorated baskets make an especially nice remembrance of summer at Christmas. Each packet is filled with the potpourri and then finished with several cinnamon sticks, hemlock cones or miniature pinecones, and dried orange peel.

The baskets are decorated with cinnamon sticks, artificial birds, cones, and ribbons.

Potpourri should be stirred from time to time to release its smells. It may be stored and brought out each year as the Christmas season approaches. It will last for many years, but needs to have essential oils added to refresh its scent.

Harrington potpourri

WINTER

The Harrington House Inn

Christmas Dinner with the Family

Cranberry Raspberry Kir

Country Ham and Crabmeat with Béarnaise
and Red Caviar

* * *

Standing Rib Roast with Beaujolais Sauce

Confetti Rice

Artichokes with Matchstick Vegetables

* * *

Miniature Fruitcake Cookies

Fresh Coconut Cake with Rum and
Orange Filling

Serves 10–12 people

Cranberry Raspberry Kir

Although this recipe uses a whole package of cranberries, one would never use that much just for making the aperitif. Make the sauce and purée one-half; use the rest as a regular cranberry sauce for the holidays.

2 bottles (750 ml) champagne

12 ounces cranberries

1 cup water

1 cup sugar

pinch of salt

1 orange rind, grated

1 10-ounce package frozen raspberries

1 ounce Grand Marnier or Triple Sec

1. Wash and pick over the cranberries, discarding the bruised or unusable ones.
2. Bring water, sugar, and salt to a boil and add the cranberries and orange rind. Cook over medium heat about 10 minutes until the berries burst. Cool slightly, divide in half, and purée. Set half of the sauce aside for another use.
3. Thaw raspberries and put through sieve to remove seeds. Add purée and Grand Marnier. Chill.
4. Place 1½ teaspoons cranberry raspberry purée in the bottom of each of the champagne flutes. Slowly fill with champagne.

Yields 2½ cups

For a variation, another time add Grand Marnier to taste to the cranberry purée and freeze in ice cube trays. Put two cubes in the bottom of a large balloon glass and fill with white wine.

Cranberry Raspberry Sherbet

Use the whole recipe (minus the champagne) as a base for cranberry raspberry sherbet.

Thin the base recipe with 2 cups orange juice and ½ cup heavy cream. Freeze in an ice cream machine. Garnish with fresh raspberries.

There is an excellent recipe for béarnaise sauce on p. 84 of Mastering the Art of French Cooking, *Volume I*, *by Julia Child, Louisette Bertholle, and Simone Beck. Ms. Child comments that making the sauce in a blender is well within the capabilities of an eight-year-old child.*

Country Ham and Crabmeat with Béarnaise and Red Caviar

A good-quality bread is essential for this first course. Red caviar makes a nice touch for holiday entertaining.

> 12 slices white bread
> (Pepperidge Farm preferred)
>
> 4 tablespoons butter
>
> 1 pound backfin crabmeat
>
> 4 tablespoons lemon juice
>
> 12 thin slices Virginia country ham
>
> ¾ cup béarnaise sauce
>
> 4 ounces red caviar

1. Using a large biscuit cutter, cut the bread into round shapes. Melt butter in a large skillet and coat both sides of each piece of bread. Fry until golden brown and set aside on paper towels to crisp.
2. Pick over the crabmeat to remove any pieces of shell or cartilage. Toss with lemon juice.
3. To serve, top each bread crouton with a tiny amount of béarnaise and a thin slice of ham. Divide the crabmeat evenly, placing it over the ham. Spoon béarnaise sauce on top and sprinkle with caviar.

12 portions

Standing Rib Roast with Beaujolais Sauce

1 4-rib standing rib roast

½ teaspoon salt, freshly ground pepper

½ cup red wine vinegar

½ cup Beaujolais wine

1 cup heavy cream

1 recipe Artichokes with Matchstick Vegetables
  (p. 208)

1. Preheat oven to 325°.
2. Place roast fat side up in a shallow pan. Sprinkle with salt and pepper. Insert a meat thermometer into the center of the roast (being careful not to let the tip touch bone) and roast uncovered. Allow 22–24 minutes per pound for medium-rare doneness.
3. Remove roast from oven and let sit for 15 minutes to firm before carving.
4. Pour fat out of pan, leaving 1–2 tablespoons drippings. Deglaze the pan by pouring in the red wine vinegar, stirring, and boiling to reduce until 2 tablespoons remain.
5. Add the wine and simmer until it is reduced by half. Blend in heavy cream. Correct the seasoning by adding salt and freshly ground pepper.
6. To serve, slice the meat and arrange on a platter. Ladle half the sauce across the middle of the meat and pass the rest in a gravy container. Surround the roast with artichoke bottoms and glazed vegetables.

10–12 portions

Roasting Beef

Roast beef at 325°. Allow 20–22 minutes per pound for rare (140°), 24–27 minutes per pound for medium (160°), 29–32 minutes per pound for well-done (170°). A standing rib roast yields 2–3 servings per pound.

Confetti Rice

3 cups beef broth

1½ cups rice

4 tablespoons butter

1 medium-size onion, chopped

1 clove garlic, minced

¼ cup yellow bell pepper, minced

¼ cup red bell pepper, minced

¼ cup green bell pepper, minced

¼ teaspoon salt, freshly ground pepper

1 tablespoon fresh parsley

1 teaspoon dried thyme

1 teaspoon dried marjoram

¼ cup heavy cream

2 eggs

⅔ cup parmesan cheese, freshly grated

1. Preheat oven to 375°.
2. Bring the beef broth to a boil and cook the rice 16–18 minutes until all the liquid is absorbed.
3. Melt 3 tablespoons butter in a large skillet and cook the onion and garlic over medium heat for about 5 minutes until the onion is translucent but not browned. Add the peppers and continue cooking for another 5 minutes.
4. Combine the rice and onion mixtures and season with salt and pepper. Mince the parsley with the dried herbs and blend with the rice mixture. Turn the mixture into a 2-quart porcelain dish that has been greased with a portion of the remaining butter.
5. Pour heavy cream over the top and bake for 5 minutes at 375°. Beat the eggs until frothy, add the parmesan cheese, and pour over the rice. Dot with paper-thin slices of butter. Bake an additional 15 minutes until the top surface has turned golden.

10–12 portions

Winter Flower Arrangement
Herb Swag

Elements in this arrangement are gathered in the autumn, when herbs are picked before frost and dried in bunches.

The base of the swag is a 12-foot-long piece of running cedar. Green glycerized galax leaves can be purchased from a florist, or fresh ones may be used. Arrange the dried herbs in clusters, using the galax as a base. Tie clusters together with flexible wire and wire them to the running cedar swag at spaced intervals.

Components used are:

Running cedar
Galax leaves
Cinnamon sticks
Statice
Dried scented geraniums (3 kinds)
Yarrow
Lemon verbena
Pineapple sage
Southern wormwood
Lamb's ear
Mint (orange mint, peppermint, spearmint)

An unexpected bonus is that most of the herbs are from the fragrance garden and have a delightful smell as one draws near.

At Fearrington House the swag is used in conjunction with a purchased balsam wreath to which cinnamon sticks and clusters of fragrance herbs are attached. Artificial birds with nests are wired in place and grosgrain ribbons complete the arrangement.

Herb Swag

It is important that all the vegetables be cut to approximately the same size so that they may be cooked in the same amount of time.

The country ham adds an extra flavor to the vegetables, but should not be repeated in the menu if the first course is used. Another option is crisply fried chopped bacon added just before serving.

Artichokes with Matchstick Vegetables

12 fresh artichokes

1 lemon, cut in half

3 tablespoons butter

3 leeks, thinly sliced

2 cloves garlic, minced

2 carrots, cut into matchstick pieces 1½″ long

1 red bell pepper, diced

2 parsnips, cut into matchstick pieces

2 tablespoons fresh parsley

½ teaspoon dried thyme

2 yellow crookneck squash, diced

½ teaspoon salt, freshly ground pepper

1 orange rind, grated

optional: ¼ cup finely shredded country ham

1. Remove the stem by breaking it at the base of the artichoke. One by one remove the leaves by bending them until they snap. Cut away the center cone of leaves and remove the fuzzy choke inside. Trim off the rough parts remaining on the bottom of the artichoke and rub all cut surfaces with lemon juice. Drop each artichoke bottom in a large bowl of water to which lemon juice has been added to keep it from discoloring while the others are being prepared.

2. Bring water to a boil in a large stockpot and simmer the artichoke bottoms for about 15 minutes until they are just tender when pierced with a knife. Allow the artichokes to cool in their cooking water. (They may be stored in this fashion overnight or until serving time to keep them from turning dark.)

3. Preheat oven to 325°.

4. Melt the butter in a large skillet and add the leeks and garlic. Cook over moderate heat for about 5 minutes until the leeks are transparent but not browned. Blend in the carrots, bell pepper, and parsnips and continue cooking until they are crispy tender. Mince the parsley with the dried thyme. Add the herbs, squash, salt, pepper, and orange rind, and cook for a few minutes until the squash is soft. Add salt and pepper.

5. If the artichokes are completely cooled, warm them covered at 325° for 10–15 minutes before serving.

6. Place the artichoke bottoms around the roast and top each with the sautéed vegetables and country ham.

12 portions

Miniature Fruitcake Cookies

As a variation this dough can be baked in 1 ½" muffin tins to yield about 3 dozen miniature muffins. Bake at 325° for about 25 minutes.

3 cups unbleached flour, sifted

1 pound candied pineapple, chopped

½ pound candied cherries, chopped

½ pound pecans, chopped

1 pound white raisins

½ cup butter

1 cup brown sugar (well-packed)

4 eggs

1 teaspoon baking soda

½ teaspoon nutmeg

3 tablespoons buttermilk

2 tablespoons bourbon

1½ teaspoons vanilla

1. Preheat oven to 325°.
2. Mix ½ cup flour with the fruits, nuts, and raisins; set aside.
3. Cream butter and sugar. Add eggs one at a time and mix well. Sift remaining 2½ cups flour, soda, and nutmeg together and add alternately with the liquids (buttermilk, bourbon, and vanilla), beginning and ending with the dry ingredients. Add fruit and mix well.
4. Chill the dough in the refrigerator at least 1 hour before cooking.
5. Drop dough by the spoonful on a well-greased cookie sheet. Bake at 325° for 15 minutes.

Yields approximately 6 dozen 2" cookies

Fresh Coconut

Drive a nail in the end of a coconut and drain the milk from it. Put the coconut in a 350° oven for 20–25 minutes until the outer shell cracks. This process allows the meat to be removed from the dark brown shell in a much easier manner. Cut the meat into chunks and grate it in a food processor.

Fresh Coconut Cake with Rum and Orange Filling

A coconut cake is a traditional holiday dessert in the South. This cake's delicious flavor comes from including grated orange rind in the batter, orange juice and rum on the layers, and an orange filling between the layers. It may be made well in advance and frozen.

¾ cup butter, softened	¼ teaspoon salt
1½ cups sugar	¾ cup milk
2 egg yolks	3 egg whites
2 cups flour	1 orange rind, grated
2 teaspoons baking powder	

* * *

¼ cup orange juice	½ cup rum

* * *

1 cup sugar	2 tablespoons butter
¼ teaspoon salt	1 orange rind, grated
4 tablespoons cornstarch	2 tablespoons lemon juice
1 cup orange juice	

* * *

8 ounces heavy cream	⅓ cup sugar
2 teaspoons rum	grated meat of 1 fresh coconut

1. Preheat oven to 350°. Grease the bottoms of two 9″ cake pans. Cut wax paper to fit the bottoms, and grease and flour the wax paper.
2. Cream the butter and sugar until light and fluffy. Beat in egg yolks one at a time. Sift the flour, baking powder, and salt together. Add alternately with milk, beginning and ending with dry ingredients.
3. Whip egg whites until stiff but not dry. Fold into the cake batter along with the grated orange rind.
4. Pour the batter into the pans and bake at 350° for about 25 minutes or until a toothpick inserted in the middle comes out clean. Let the cakes cool in the pans for a few minutes, invert onto rack, and peel off the wax paper.

5. Slice the layers in half to get 4 thin layers, prick with a fork, and drizzle with the mixture of orange juice and rum. Set aside.

6. Blend 1 cup sugar with salt and cornstarch until the mixture is smooth. Gradually add orange juice and bring to a boil on top of the stove. Boil 1–2 minutes, remove from the heat, and stir in butter, orange rind, and lemon juice. Cool. Spread ⅓ of the mixture on the first layer; stack the second and third layers and repeat the process. Add the fourth layer.

7. Whip the cream until soft peaks form and add the rum and sugar. Continue to whip until stiff. Spread over the cake and pat shredded coconut onto the sides and top.

Yields one 4-layer 9″ cake

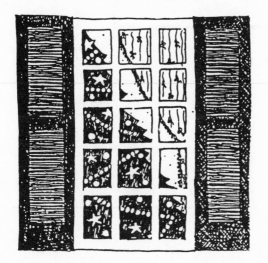

New Year's Eve

Champagne

White Wine over Cassis Ice

Miniature Biscuits with Country Ham

Cheese Wafers with Pecans

*   *   *

Mussel Soup with Red Pepper Cream

*   *   *

Pink Grapefruit Vodka Sorbet

*   *   *

Roast Tenderloin of Beef with Madeira Sauce

Glazed Carrots, Turnips, and Chestnuts

Acorn Squash with Spinach Soufflé

*   *   *

Walnut Lace Tart

Serves 6 people

Miniature Biscuits with Country Ham

1¼ cups flour

¾ teaspoon baking powder

¼ teaspoon baking soda

1 tablespoon sugar

¾ teaspoon salt

¼ cup shortening

¾ teaspoon yeast

½ cup buttermilk

2¼ teaspoons warm water

2 ounces country ham, thinly sliced

2–3 tablespoons honeycup mustard

1. Preheat oven to 450°.
2. Sift flour, baking powder, soda, sugar, and salt into a bowl. Cut the shortening into the mixture until it is the consistency of meal.
3. Dissolve yeast in warm water and make certain it is active before adding it along with the buttermilk to the flour and shortening.
4. Mix together until smooth. Turn out on a lightly floured surface and knead for 2–3 minutes. Roll to a thickness of ½". Cut the biscuits with a 1¼" cookie cutter, set 1" apart on an ungreased baking sheet, cover, and let rise for 30 minutes. Bake at 450° for 10 minutes.
5. Split each biscuit, spread with honeycup mustard, add a thin slice of country ham, and replace top.

Yields approximately 34 miniature biscuits

Herbed Biscuits

1 tablespoon parsley, minced

1½ teaspoons chives, minced

Chop the herbs together and add to the flour and shortening in step 2. Continue the recipe as directed.

The recipe for Cheese Wafers will be found on p. 72.

Cassis Ice Cubes

½ cup cassis

½ cup water

Mix together and freeze in an ice tray. Place one cube in the bottom of a large balloon wine glass and gently pour white wine or champagne over.

Winter Flower Arrangement
Winter Basket

By purchasing a few inexpensive plants (in this case one azalea and two primroses) and gathering from one's own collection it is possible to have a basket of spring flowers in January.

All the plants are in pots or containers. The basket is lined and padded with plastic to bring all plant material to the same level.

The paper-whites are plucked from a grouping of forced bulbs. Since they are shallow-rooted, they are easy to remove and are not harmed by being disturbed. These are placed in a small container with rocks around the bulbs to stabilize them.

It is possible to keep the arrangement going for quite some time by removing faded plants and replacing them with fresh ones.

Components used are:

Ivy
Primroses
Maidenhair fern
Paper-whites
Azalea
African violets
Gray moss from the woods

Mussel Soup with Red Pepper Cream

2 ribs celery, chopped

4 shallots, chopped

bouquet garni (parsley sprigs, bay leaf, thyme sprigs)

1 cup dry white wine

4 pounds mussels, scrubbed and debearded

3–4 leeks, trimmed, washed, and sliced

2 ounces unsalted butter

$\frac{5}{8}$ gram thread saffron; reserve a few threads for garnish

8 ounces bottled clam juice or fish fumet

3 cups heavy cream

½ teaspoon salt, freshly ground pepper

1 recipe Red Pepper Cream

1. Combine celery, shallots, bouquet garni, wine, and mussels in a large casserole or stockpot. Bring to a boil and simmer, covered, shaking the pan occasionally, until all mussels are open.
2. Remove mussels. Discard shells and reserve them for garnish, if desired. Strain liquid through a fine strainer or cheesecloth.
3. In a covered heavy-bottomed stockpot, cook leeks in butter over low heat for 5–8 minutes until they are very soft but not browned. Stir in saffron and cook for 2 minutes. Add clam juice, simmer gently for 10 minutes, and purée in a food processor or blender. Return the mixture to the saucepan, add cream, bring to a simmer, and season with salt and pepper.
4. To serve, reheat soup and ladle into 6 bowls. Add 6–8 mussels to each bowl. Place a tablespoon or two of the red pepper cream in the center and sprinkle a few saffron threads on each.

6 portions

Ben Barker

Red Pepper Cream

1 large sweet red pepper, roasted, peeled,
   and puréed in the blender

2 egg yolks, room temperature

2 tablespoons orange juice

Tabasco

½ teaspoon salt, freshly ground pepper

¼ cup heavy cream, whipped to soft peaks

Combine pepper, egg yolks, orange juice, Tabasco, salt, and pepper in a large stainless bowl over simmering water. Over moderate heat, whisk with a balloon whip until light and frothy. Continue whisking until mixture thickens and you can see the bottom of the bowl; avoid overcooking and scrambling eggs. Remove from heat, cool completely, and fold in whipped cream. Refrigerate until needed.

Yields approximately ½ cup

Ben Barker

Roasted Red Bell Peppers

There are two methods of roasting bell peppers.

One is to roast them on top of a gas range over an open flame. Place one pepper on each eye and turn each one frequently with tongs until the skin is black and blistered.

The other is to roast them in a 500° oven. Place the peppers on a baking sheet inside the oven and turn them frequently until all surfaces are blackened.

After using either method, seal the peppers in a paper bag to cool. When they are cool, rub off their skins, cut peppers in half, remove seeds and ribs, and purée in a food processor.

Pink Grapefruit Vodka Sorbet

1 cup sugar

1 cup water

2 cups pink grapefruit juice

1/4 cup vodka

2 tablespoons cream

1/2 tablespoon grenadine syrup

Combine sugar and water to make a sugar syrup. Blend in the rest of the ingredients, mix well, and chill completely. Freeze.

Yields six 1/2-cup servings

Karen Barker

Roast Tenderloin of Beef with Madeira Sauce

1 beef tenderloin, 5½–6 pounds, trimmed of all fat

½ teaspoon salt, freshly ground pepper

2 tablespoons dijon mustard

4 ounces bacon, diced, fried, and drained

5½ ounces mushrooms, sliced and with stems removed

2 cloves garlic, minced

1 shallot, minced

3 tablespoons peanut oil

1 cup fresh orange juice

1 cup Madeira

½ cup ruby port

¼ cup brandy

2 cups brown beef stock or beef broth

1 cup heavy cream

4 tablespoons butter, softened

optional: watercress for garnish

1. Preheat oven to 450°.
2. Make a 2″ deep incision the length of the roast so that the meat opens and lies flat. Salt and pepper the inside and spread with dijon mustard.
3. Sauté the mushrooms for 1 minute in the pan in which the bacon was cooked. Add garlic and the shallot and continue to cook for another minute. Combine with bacon and spread the mixture down the middle of the roast. Roll the tenderloin to its original shape and tie it with butcher's twine at 1″ intervals.
4. Heat the peanut oil to the smoking point in a skillet large enough to accommodate the roast. Add the roast and sear it on all sides until nicely browned. Remove it and place it seam side up in a roasting pan with a rack. The roast may be prepared to this point earlier in the day and set aside, covered, at room temperature until it is ready to be finished.
5. Combine orange juice, Madeira, port, and brandy in a saucepan and bring to a boil. Simmer until reduced by half. Add beef stock and reduce again by half. Add cream and reduce by half. Set aside.
6. Put the roast in a 450° oven and reduce the temperature to 375°. Roast 15–18 minutes (total cooking time for medium-rare). Remove and allow roast to sit for 5 minutes.
7. Bring sauce to a boil and adjust seasoning. Remove from the heat and whisk in the butter 1 tablespoon at a time.
8. Slice beef in ½″ slices and arrange on a platter with vegetables. Nap with the sauce and garnish with watercress.

6–8 portions

Ben Barker

Glazed Carrots, Turnips, and Chestnuts

½ pound carrots

½ pound turnips

6 ounces butter

2 tablespoons brown sugar

¼ cup canned chestnuts

freshly grated nutmeg

1. Peel the carrots and turnips and slice into ⅛″ rounds. Cook in boiling salted water until crispy tender, and refresh under cold running water.
2. Melt butter in a skillet and add brown sugar, turnips, and carrots. Toss to make certain all surfaces are covered. Cook until brown sugar has dissolved and has made a glaze for the vegetables.
3. Drain the chestnuts, cut them into matchstick pieces, and add them to the pan to heat through.
4. Grate fresh nutmeg over the top of the vegetables and mix before serving.

6 portions

Rice with Scallions and Chives

3 cups water

1½ cups rice

2 tablespoons butter

⅓ cup parmesan cheese, freshly grated

freshly ground pepper

4 scallions, minced

3 tablespoons chives, minced

Bring the water to a boil and cook the rice, covered, over medium heat for about 18 minutes until all the water is absorbed.

Blend in the butter and parmesan and stir until the butter is melted. Add pepper, scallions, and chives.

6–8 portions

Acorn Squash with Spinach Soufflé

3 small acorn squash, 3½″ in diameter

1 tablespoon butter

½ teaspoon salt, freshly ground pepper

freshly grated nutmeg

* * *

1½ tablespoons butter

1½ tablespoons flour

¼ teaspoon dry mustard

pinch of cayenne pepper

¼ teaspoon salt

½ cup milk, heated almost to the boiling point

2 egg yolks

* * *

1 teaspoon butter

2 tablespoons scallions, minced

½ cup spinach, cooked, squeezed dry, and chopped

3 egg whites

½ cup parmesan cheese, freshly grated

1. Preheat oven to 375°.
2. Cut the squash in half and remove the seeds. Melt 1 tablespoon butter and brush all cut surfaces. Season with salt, pepper, and nutmeg. Arrange cut side up in a baking dish. Cover with foil and bake for 35 minutes until the flesh is tender when pierced with a fork. Remove from the oven and set aside.
3. Raise oven temperature to 400°.
4. Melt 1½ tablespoons butter in a saucepan and blend in the flour, mustard, cayenne, and salt. Cook over medium heat for 2 minutes without browning. Pour in the hot milk all at once, stir vigorously with a whisk, and cook until thickened. Remove from heat and add the egg yolks.
5. Melt 1 teaspoon butter in a small skillet, add the scallions, and cook for 2–3 minutes. Add the chopped spinach and blend the whole mixture into the soufflé base.
6. Beat the egg whites with salt until stiff and stir about ⅓ of the whites into the base to lighten it. Quickly blend in the grated cheese and the rest of the whites.
7. Divide the soufflé mixture among the 6 squash halves, filling each almost full. Set in a large baking dish and place in the oven. Turn the temperature down to 375° and bake for 20 minutes. Remove from the oven and serve immediately.

6 portions

Walnut Lace Tart

1 partially baked 11″ Orange Pastry Shell

2 large eggs

¼ cup plus 2 tablespoons sugar

¾ cup light corn syrup

2 ounces unsalted butter, melted

1 tablespoon Grand Marnier

1 teaspoon vanilla

1 tablespoon orange rind, finely chopped

2 cups walnuts, coarsely chopped

2½ ounces semisweet chocolate

2 tablespoons Grand Marnier

8 ounces heavy cream, whipped and
   lightly sweetened

1. Preheat oven to 350°.
2. Combine eggs with sugar until well blended. Add corn syrup,
   butter, 1 tablespoon Grand Marnier, vanilla, orange rind, and
   walnuts. Stir to mix well.
3. Pour into prepared pastry shell, distributing nuts evenly.
4. Bake at 350° for about 40 minutes until mixture is just set in the
   center. Remove tart and cool on rack.
5. Melt semisweet chocolate in a double boiler. Cool slightly. Form
   a cone out of parchment paper and fill with melted chocolate.
   Cut off tip to form a pin-size opening and pipe chocolate over
   the tart in a zigzagging lacy pattern. Chill briefly to harden
   chocolate.
6. Serve at room temperature with Grand Marnier flavored whipped
   cream.

Yields one 11″ tart

Karen Barker

If there is no parchment paper in your kitchen, simply drizzle chocolate over the tart using a fork.

Orange Pastry Shell

1½ cups flour

1 tablespoon sugar

¼ teaspoon salt

1 teaspoon orange rind, finely chopped

4 ounces butter

2 ounces shortening

1 tablespoon Grand Marnier

3–4 tablespoons cold water

1. Combine flour, sugar, salt, and orange rind. Cut in butter and shortening until the mixture has the texture of coarse crumbs.
2. Add Grand Marnier and cold water, tossing and stirring to distribute until the mixture starts to clean the sides of the bowl and a dough is formed. Refrigerate until thoroughly chilled.
3. Roll dough out to fit an 11″ tart pan with a removable bottom. Chill pastry shell several hours.
4. Preheat oven to 400°. Pierce bottom of shell several times with a fork. Line shell with parchment paper and weight with dried beans or rice. Bake at 400° for 10 minutes. Remove parchment and beans and bake about 5 minutes more until very lightly browned. Prick dough if it bubbles up.

Yields one 11″ pastry shell

Karen Barker

Winter Get-Together

Hearty Vegetable Soup

Chili

Slaw

Hoppin' John

Spoonbread with Country Ham

*   *   *

Lemon Chess Tart

Bourbon Balls

Serves 6–8 people

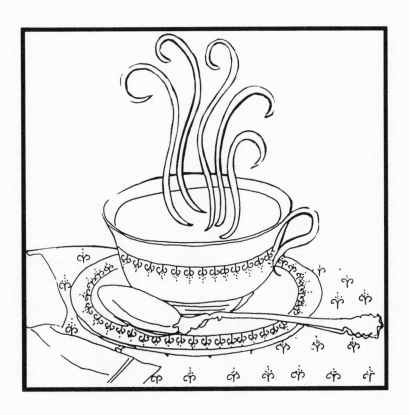

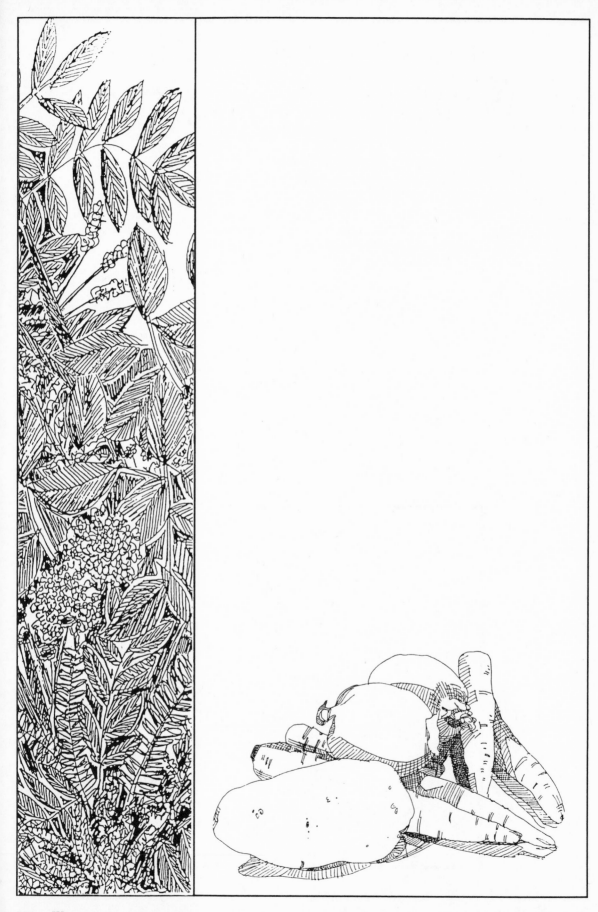

Hearty Vegetable Soup

This wonderful soup is a favorite of every member of our family, being especially welcome on a cold winter night. It needs to be started one day, left to sit overnight, and finished the next day. The consistency should be thick. It freezes beautifully.

3 pounds lean stew beef, cut in small pieces

3 marrow bones

2½–3 quarts water

2 cans beef bouillon

1 potato, diced

5 onions, chopped

3 carrots, diced

2 ribs celery, diced

6 cups canned tomatoes

½ cup dried beans

1½ teaspoons salt, freshly ground pepper

¾ cup frozen baby lima beans

¾ cup frozen green peas

¾ cup frozen corn

½ cup okra, sliced

1. Put beef and soupbones in a large pot with enough water to cover. Bring to a boil and simmer for several hours.
2. Remove from the stove and let come to room temperature. Set in a cool place overnight so that the fat will come to the top surface and solidify.
3. The next day, remove the surface fat. Bring to a boil again and add bouillon, potato, onions, carrots, celery, canned tomatoes, and dried beans. Simmer for several hours. Salt and pepper to taste. Skim froth several times during the cooking process. Thirty minutes before serving add the lima beans, peas, corn, and okra.

8–10 portions

Winter is a time for having sugarplums (ours consist of candied orange peel, a strawberry dipped in chocolate, toasted pecans, and a tiny cookie), mulled wines, hearty soups for lunch, and homemade breads. It is a time to have friends over for tea in the afternoon. And it is a time to begin perusing the seed catalogs for spring.

Winter Flower Arranging Tip

Freesias

If you are lucky enough to have an arrangement of freesias, be sure to save them as the arrangement fades because the flowers keep their bright color as they dry. Piled loosely in a dark bowl to set off the color, they brighten a winter day and remind us that spring is not too far behind.

Chili

This is a good recipe to double and freeze half for use another time. It is seasoned just right but is only moderately hot; to make it more so, simply increase the amounts of chili powder and cayenne.

1½ pounds ground beef

2 medium-size onions, diced

2 ribs celery, chopped

1 clove garlic, minced

1 green pepper, diced

1 large can (1 lb, 13 oz.) tomatoes

2 small bay leaves

2 teaspoons salt

1–2 tablespoons chili powder

½ teaspoon dried thyme

⅛ teaspoon paprika

½ teaspoon dried oregano

⅛ teaspoon cayenne pepper

1 15½-ounce can kidney beans, drained (with juice reserved)

optional:
  ½ avocado, sliced
  1 cup cheddar cheese, grated
  1–2 dried hot peppers, finely minced

1. Brown beef in a skillet. Add onion, celery, garlic, and green pepper and cook for several minutes until crispy tender. Drain tomatoes (save liquid), deseed, and cut into small strips. Add to the beef mixture along with all the seasonings.
2. Cover and simmer for 1½ hours. From time to time add small amounts of tomato juice plus the liquid from the kidney beans so that the consistency is like that of a heavy soup.
3. When ready to serve, add the kidney beans to heat through. Garnish with sliced avocado, grated cheese, and/or minced hot peppers.

8–10 portions

Hoppin' John

There is an old Southern tradition of serving Hoppin' John on New Year's Day to bring good luck. In one family I know of there was a related tradition: when the children were told Hoppin' John would be served, they all jumped up from the table and hopped around it!

This is an updated version of the original Hoppin' John. It should not be reserved just for New Year's Day.

8 ounces dried black-eyed peas	1 cup raw rice
4 ounces bacon	2 cups water
3 tablespoons olive oil	⅓ cup red bell pepper, minced
1½ onions, chopped	⅓ cup green pepper, minced
1 tablespoon salt, freshly ground pepper	¼ cup scallions, minced
	½ cup parmesan cheese
1 teaspoon butter	

1. Soak peas overnight in a large bowl with water to cover. Drain.
2. Fry the bacon crisp and set aside to drain. Reserve 2 tablespoons of the drippings and place them with olive oil in a large skillet. Cook the onions over medium heat for about 8 minutes or until translucent but not browned.
3. Place peas in a large Dutch oven with enough water to cover, and add the onion mixture (be careful to get all the flavoring oils). Add salt and pepper. Bring to a boil and then reduce heat to a slow simmer for 40–45 minutes. Add more water during the cooking process if necessary. At the end of cooking time, the water should be almost all absorbed and the peas should be tender.
4. Bring 2 cups of water to a boil; if any liquid remains from the black-eyed peas, substitute it for water and the results will be much more flavorful. Add the butter and 1 cup rice. Cook 18–20 minutes until tender.
5. Combine the peas and rice, heat through, and serve. Garnish with crumbled bacon, minced peppers, scallions, and parmesan cheese.

6–8 portions

Winter Flower Arranging Tip
African Violets

African violets are inexpensive, and just a few go a long way toward cheering things up in the middle of winter. One good way to display them is to line a flat basket with plastic, add several violets in their pots, and fill in all the empty spaces with gray Spanish moss.

Spoonbread with Country Ham

We always have plenty of country ham in our kitchen, and use it freely as a garnish or to add extra flavor. Alternatively, substitute crumbled fried bacon.

1 cup cornmeal

1 teaspoon salt

1 tablespoon sugar

1 egg, beaten

½ teaspoon baking soda

1 cup buttermilk

1½ tablespoons shortening

1½ ounces country ham, minced

1. Preheat oven to 400°.
2. Pour ¾ cup boiling water over the cornmeal in a bowl, stir, cover, and let cool. Mix in the salt, sugar, and egg. Dissolve soda in buttermilk and beat into the mixture along with the shortening and ham.
3. Pour into a greased 11¼″ × 7½″ baking dish and bake at 400° for 30 minutes.
4. To serve, "spoon" the bread from the baking pan. Or, if you prefer, bake it 5 minutes longer and cut it into squares.

8 portions

Lemon Chess Tart

1 unbaked 9″ pie shell (recipe p. 100)

1 tablespoon flour

1 tablespoon cornmeal

1½ cups sugar

3 eggs, lightly beaten

3 tablespoons butter, melted

3 tablespoons milk

¼ cup lemon juice

1 lemon rind, grated

8 ounces heavy cream, whipped and sweetened

1 kiwi

1. Preheat oven to 375°.
2. Mix flour, cornmeal, and sugar together and add to eggs. Add butter, milk, lemon juice, and lemon rind and pour into unbaked pie shell. (For a more elegant presentation, make individual tarts.) Bake at 375° for 35–40 minutes.
3. Serve with sweetened whipped cream and garnish with kiwi fruit slices or candied lemon peel. In the spring garnish with mint leaves or fresh violets and violet leaves.

6–8 portions

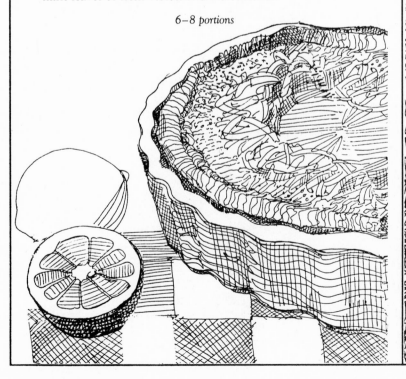

Winter Flower Arrangement
Carnations and Lilies

At certain times of the year one is willing to be extravagant in the purchase of flowers. Christmas is one of those times.

This arrangement uses one bunch of 25 stems of carnations and one bunch of 10 stems of lilies. The rest comes from the yard. All are arranged in soaked oasis in a tin can with water.

Components used are:

Carnations
Lilies
Cedar foliage
Deodora cedar
Galax
Holly

Bourbon Balls

30 vanilla wafers, ground to fine crumbs

2½ tablespoons cocoa powder

2¼ tablespoons light corn syrup

⅓ cup pecans, finely ground

4 tablespoons bourbon

confectioners' sugar

Combine vanilla wafer crumbs, cocoa, corn syrup, pecans, and bourbon and mix until well combined. Form into small balls (approximately ½ tablespoon each). Roll balls in powdered sugar and store in an airtight container at room temperature for 48 hours before serving.

Roll the balls in powdered sugar again before serving.

Yields approximately 2 dozen

Karen Barker

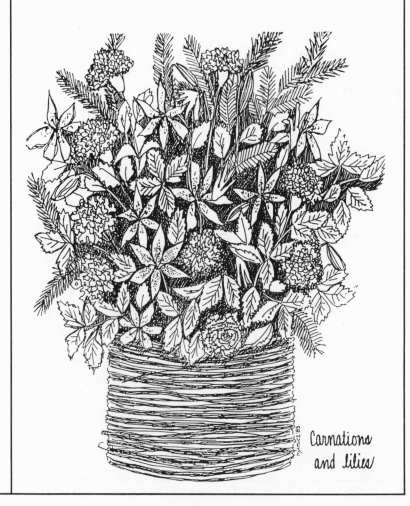

Carnations and lilies

Groundhog Day Lunch

Chicken Pot Pie

Fearrington House Chicken Country Captain

Black-eyed Peas with Rosemary

Broccoli with Sesame Seeds

*　　*　　*

Banana Fritters with Orange Sauce

Serves 6–8 people

Chicken Pot Pie

Mama Nell says this is the way *real* Southern cooks make chicken pot pie. No vegetables are served—just the chicken, its thickened stock, and pastry on the top that bakes to a beautiful golden brown.

1 recipe Pot Pie Pastry

1 roasting chicken, 3½–4 pounds

2 ribs celery

1 carrot

1 small onion, quartered

½ teaspoon salt

4 tablespoons butter

4 tablespoons flour

2 cups chicken stock

1 egg yolk

1 teaspoon water

1. Place the chicken, celery, carrot, and onion in a large stockpot. Add 3–4 cups of water plus salt to taste. Bring to a boil and simmer for 2 hours or until tender. Cool the meat, debone it, and cut it into bite-size pieces. Set aside. Chill stock and skim off fat.
2. Preheat oven to 425°.
3. Melt butter in a medium-size saucepan. Add flour, cook, and stir for 2 minutes. Add fat-free chicken stock, stirring constantly until thick and smooth.
4. Place chicken in 1½-quart oval baking dish and cover with thickened broth. Roll pastry to fit, cut vents for steam, and brush with egg yolk glaze (made by mixing egg yolk and water together). Bake at 425° for 25–30 minutes until golden brown.

6–8 portions

Pot Pie Pastry

Cut ½ stick butter into 1 cup flour with pastry blender until the butter is the size of small peas. Sprinkle with 2 tablespoons water and mix with a fork until the mixture can be formed into a ball. Cover and chill for at least 30 minutes before rolling.

Miniature Biscuits with Country Ham (recipe p. 215) and Glazed Baby Carrots (recipe p. 35) go very well with the recipes on the Groundhog Day Lunch menu.

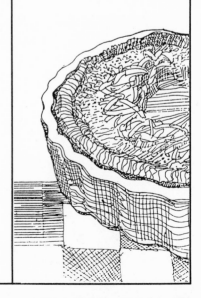

Broccoli with Sesame Seeds

1 head broccoli

4 tablespoons butter, melted

2 tablespoons lemon juice

2 tablespoons toasted sesame seeds

Wash the broccoli and separate in flowerettes. Cook in rapidly boiling water for about 3 minutes until crispy tender. Drain and refresh under cold water to set the bright green color.

Just before serving toss with melted butter, lemon juice, and sesame seeds. (The lemon juice will discolor the broccoli if allowed to sit for a long period of time.)

6–8 portions

Black-Eyed Peas with Rosemary

Use the recipe on p. 110 for the proportions and procedure for black-eyed peas. Substitute 3 sprigs of minced fresh rosemary for the herbes de Provence.

Corn Chowder with Red Bell Peppers *

4 ounces salt pork

1 medium-size onion, finely diced

2½ ounces flour

6 cups chicken stock

¼ teaspoon oregano

1 12-ounce can creamed corn

1 pound potatoes, peeled and cut into ¼" cubes

4 ears fresh corn

1 pint heavy cream

1 teaspoon salt, freshly ground black pepper

3 ounces red bell pepper, diced

4 scallions, minced

1. Render salt pork until lightly browned. Add onion and cook for about 10 minutes until translucent but not browned.
2. Stir in flour and cook over low heat 3–5 minutes without browning. Blend in chicken stock, add oregano, and bring to a boil.
3. Add creamed corn and bring slowly to a boil, stirring. Strain through a coarse sieve, pressing on solids. Return to range.
4. Add potatoes and cook 10 minutes. Cut the corn from the ears, add to the soup, and simmer for about 10 more minutes until potatoes are done.
5. Blend in heavy cream, bring to a simmer, and season well (should be peppery). Garnish with diced red pepper and minced scallions.

6–8 portions

Ben Barker

* Extra Recipe

Fearrington House Chicken Country Captain

In many recipes for country captain the chicken is first stewed and the meat is then chopped into small pieces. In ours, chicken pieces are first sautéed and then baked. Either way the results produce a delicious meal for an American tradition: Groundhog Day.

4 chicken breasts, each cut in half

8 chicken legs

3 tablespoons peanut oil

1 large onion, peeled and sliced

2 green bell peppers, sliced

2 cloves garlic, minced

1 8-ounce can tomatoes, drained, deseeded, and chopped

freshly grated nutmeg

1 teaspoon freshly ground pepper

1 teaspoon curry (or to taste)

½ teaspoon salt

¼ cup currants

3 cups cooked rice

⅓ cup slivered almonds, toasted

2 tablespoons fresh parsley, minced

1. Preheat oven to 350°.
2. Brown the chicken breasts and legs in the peanut oil over moderate heat. Arrange to fit in a baking dish and set aside.
3. In the same skillet used to brown the chicken, sauté the onion, peppers, and garlic for about 5 minutes. Add the tomatoes, nutmeg, pepper, curry, and salt. Simmer for another 3–4 minutes.
4. Pour the tomato-onion mixture over the chicken and bake covered for 30 minutes.
5. Remove from oven and sprinkle with currants. Return to oven for an additional 15 minutes.
6. To serve, place ½ cup rice on each plate and top with a chicken leg and a piece of breast plus sauce. Garnish with toasted almonds and parsley.

6–8 portions

Another Country Captain

Use the same recipe ingredients, omitting the chicken legs and peanut oil but adding ½ cup heavy cream to the list.

Save the juice from the drained tomatoes and add ¼ cup of it to the heavy cream.

Poach the chicken breasts and cut into small pieces. Add to the tomato-onion mixture along with the thinned heavy cream. It is not necessary to bake the country captain, since the chicken is already cooked.

Sprinkle with currants and serve on top of cooked rice. Garnish with almonds and parsley.

Winter Flower Arrangement

Gladiolas, Christmas Cactus, and Lilacs

This arrangement requires an oversized basket, one big enough to contain both cut flowers and potted plants.

Arrange 15-20 gladiolas and lilacs in oasis in a large tin can filled with water. The use of soaked oasis and water often allows an arrangement to last for a week.

Line the basket with a sheet of plastic. Place the can in the middle and four pots of blooming cacti in each corner. It may be necessary to build up the corners of the basket with rolled newspaper in order to bring the potted plants to an even level with the edges of the basket. The plastic will hold water inside as the cacti are watered during the week.

For a Christmas arrangement, use red gladiolas in the middle and 4" potted white poinsettias in the corners.

Scalloped Oysters *

Substitute scalloped oysters for the country captain on another occasion to give the menu a more varied taste.

½ cup soft bread crumbs	2 tablespoons parsley, chopped
½ cup fine cracker crumbs	1 tablespoon sherry
½ stick unsalted butter, melted	¼ cup heavy cream
1 quart select oysters in their liquor	4–6 scallions, minced
¼ teaspoon salt, freshly ground pepper	6 slices bacon, fried, drained, and chopped

1. Preheat oven to 350°.
2. Mix the bread crumbs and cracker crumbs with the melted butter and set aside. Divide the oysters among eight 4-ounce ramekins, reserving the liquor. Sprinkle with salt, pepper, and parsley. Mix ⅓ cup of the oyster liquor with the sherry and heavy cream and pour over the oysters. Sprinkle with the rest of the crumb mixture.
3. Bake for about 10 minutes at 350° until the crumbs are golden brown.
4. To serve, garnish each ramekin with the scallions and bacon.

8 portions

* Extra Recipe

Banana Fritters with Orange Sauce

2 egg yolks

⅔ cup milk

1 tablespoon butter, melted

1 cup unbleached flour

¼ teaspoon salt

1 tablespoon sugar

1 tablespoon Grand Marnier

1 tablespoon orange rind, grated

2 egg whites

3 bananas

1 cup vegetable oil

confectioners' sugar

1 recipe Orange Sauce

1. Mix the egg yolks, milk, and butter. Sift the dry ingredients together and blend with the milk mixture. Add the Grand Marnier and orange rind. Refrigerate the batter for 2 hours.
2. Beat the egg whites until they hold stiff peaks. Blend into the fritter batter.
3. Slice the bananas in half lengthwise, and then slice each half crosswise into 3 pieces.
4. Heat the vegetable oil in a large skillet. Dip the banana pieces into the batter and fry until golden brown on both sides.
5. Dust with confectioners' sugar and serve immediately. Spoon the orange sauce over the top.

6–8 portions

Banana fritters are also excellent for a special-occasion breakfast. Serve them in the same manner, adding fresh raspberries and mint in the summertime for a touch of color.

For a perfect Southern breakfast, serve the fritters with chopped pecans as a garnish and honey maple syrup.

Orange Sauce

½ cup vanilla yogurt

1 tablespoon sugar

1 tablespoon Grand Marnier

1 tablespoon orange rind, grated

Mix together all the ingredients and spoon over the banana fritters.

The Harrington House Restaurant

Early March
Kite Flying

Goat Cheese Tart

Pasta Salad with Pine Nuts and Pesto

Chilled Vegetables with Lemon Thyme Mayonnaise

Assorted Stuffed Eggs

Tom Thumb Cheesecakes

Serves 6–8 people

Belted Galloway

Goat Cheese Tart

1 partially baked 11″ tart shell (recipe follows)

2 tablespoons butter

7 ounces leeks, cleaned and sliced
(do not use dark green parts)

10 ounces Montrachet chèvre cheese

2 teaspoons fresh herbs (thyme, savory,
chives, and basil), chopped

2 small scallions, sliced

1 red pepper, roasted, skin removed,
and flesh diced

4 sun-dried tomatoes, soaked in warm water
to soften, drained, and diced

4 eggs

1 cup half-and-half

½ cup heavy cream

½ teaspoon salt, freshly ground pepper

Tabasco

½ teaspoon fresh parsley, minced

1. Preheat oven to 350°.
2. Melt butter, add leeks, cover with lid or parchment paper, and cook over low heat, stirring often, until leeks are soft but not brown.
3. Evenly distribute leeks into partially baked tart shell. Cover with half the cheese crumbled evenly over surface. Sprinkle with fresh herbs, scallions, red pepper, diced tomatoes, and the remaining cheese.
4. Combine eggs with half-and-half and cream. Season to taste with salt, pepper, and Tabasco. Mix well.
5. Place shell on oven shelf. Carefully and slowly fill with custard mixture. (There may be excess custard.) Sprinkle surface with parsley. Bake at 350° for about 30–40 minutes until filling is set, slightly puffed, and just starting to turn brown.

6–8 portions

Karen Barker

Winter Greenery

Begin by collecting as many kinds of greenery as seem appropriate for winter: cedar, hollies of all descriptions, pine, magnolia, elaeagnus, deodora cedar, juniper, and boxwood. A variety of textures and shapes makes the arrangement interesting.

Condition the greens as soon as they are cut by putting them in warm water or completely submerging them in a bathtub.

Arrange the greens in a tin can in a plastic-lined basket or a deep ceramic vessel that holds water. Conditioned greens arranged in water should last for weeks.

For smaller arrangements, lesser amounts of the same kind of greens may be used with flowers. One week try pink carnations and pink snapdragons; another week try yellow gladiolas with yellow chrysanthemums. Each week dismantle the arrangement, start with fresh flowers and oasis, but use the same greens.

Winter Flower Arrangement

Cyclamen

This arrangement consists of three potted cyclamen in a slat basket lined with plastic. Stuff the area between the slats with small pieces of moss, and also the top surface of the arrangement.

The arrangement should be placed in bright natural light in a cool spot, if possible, to keep the cyclamen blooming for a long time. They will need weekly watering.

Pastry for Goat Cheese Tart

1½ cups flour

½ teaspoon salt

3 ounces butter

1½ ounces shortening

3–4 tablespoons cold water

1 egg white, lightly beaten

1. Combine flour and salt in mixing bowl. Cut in butter and shortening until the mixture resembles coarse crumbs.
2. Add cold water gradually, stirring and tossing to blend until dough begins to clean sides of the bowl and forms a ball (additional water may be necessary). Chill dough several hours.
3. Preheat oven to 425°. Lightly butter an 11″ tart pan with a removable bottom. Roll out pastry and fit into pan, forming a double edge. Chill thoroughly.
4. Prick chilled shell in several places with a fork. Line with parchment paper and weight with dried beans or rice. Bake at 425° for about 15 minutes until edges of shell start to take on color and pastry is "set" on bottom. Remove weights and paper. Turn oven down to 400° and bake pastry until shell starts to turn light brown. If pastry bubbles up, prick it.
5. Remove shell from oven and immediately brush it with lightly beaten egg white.

Yields one 11″ pastry shell

Cyclamen in a slat basket

Pasta Salad with Pine Nuts and Pesto

1 pound tortellini

2 medium-size carrots

1½ ounces black olives

2 ounces feta cheese

4–6 ounces frozen green peas, thawed

2 shallots or 4–6 scallions, minced

1 medium-size red bell pepper, diced

2 ounces country ham, minced

2 ounces pine nuts, toasted

8 ounces cherry tomatoes

1 recipe Vinaigrette (p. 33)

2 tablespoons pesto (recipe p. 138)

2–3 tablespoons mixed herbs (parsley, chives, marjoram), minced

Shell or fusilli pasta may easily be substituted for the tortellini. These pastas keep their shape and will not break apart during the mixing of the salad.

1. In a large saucepan, cook tortellini and carrots in 2 quarts water for 15–20 minutes until both are fork-tender. Drain and refresh with cold water.

2. Remove the skin of the carrots under running water and dice them. Pit the black olives and slice them into 3–4 pieces. Cut the feta cheese into ¼″ pieces. Add carrots, olives, and feta cheese to the pasta along with peas, scallions, and red pepper.

3. Mince the country ham or shred in the food processor. Add to the pasta along with toasted pine nuts, the vinaigrette, and the pesto.

4. Cut the cherry tomatoes in half and scoop out the seeds. Cut in slivers and add to tortellini mixture with the herbs. Mix well and chill until serving time.

6–8 portions

Grapevine Wreath with Flowers

Use this arrangement for the dining room table or a coffee table.

Condition the greens by submerging them in water in a bathtub overnight.

Place flowers in water vials. As the arrangement is being put together, the vials are hidden among the greens. Components used are:

White lilies
Red poinsettias
Purple freesia
Boxwood
Rosemary with its blossom
Galax leaves
Holly
Grapevine wreath
Angel-shaped Christmas candle
Vials

Purchase very special flowers for a winter occasion. Even just a few can be spectacular with native greens.

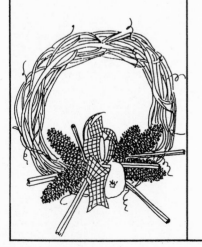

Walter's Pasta Salad *

This pasta salad and homemade bread would make a fine lunch any season of the year.

3 cups medium shell pasta, cooked and drained

¾ cup raisins

¼ cup slivered almonds, toasted

2 tablespoons mixed herbs (parsley, tarragon, chives), minced

1 recipe Vinaigrette (recipe follows)

1½ pounds small spinach leaves, washed and drained

1 red onion, sliced into rings

2 oranges, peeled and sliced

1. Combine pasta, raisins, almonds, herbs, and dressing; mix lightly.
2. Arrange spinach, onion, and oranges on a serving plate. Top with pasta mixture.
3. Sprinkle with additional herbs if desired.

8–10 portions

Walter Royal

* Extra Recipe

Vinaigrette

1 teaspoon grainy mustard   **3 tablespoons red wine vinegar**

9 tablespoons olive oil   **½ teaspoon salt**

freshly ground pepper   **2 teaspoons dijon mustard**

Dissolve the salt in the vinegar and blend in the mustards. Whisk the mixture, adding the olive oil one tablespoon at a time. Season with pepper.

Chilled Vegetables with Lemon Thyme Mayonnaise

8 ounces asparagus

8 ounces new potatoes
1–2" in diameter

4 ounces carrots

12 ounces cherry tomatoes

8 ounces sugar snap peas

1 recipe Lemon Thyme
Mayonnaise

1 red cabbage

1. Snap the stems of the asparagus; wash, drain, and cook in boiling water for about 2 minutes. Refresh under cold water to set the bright green color. Drain.
2. Cook unpeeled new potatoes for about 20 minutes until fork-tender. Drain and set aside.
3. Peel carrots and cut into matchstick pieces. Cook in boiling water for about 5 minutes until fork-tender. Drain.
4. String sugar snaps and cook no longer than 1 minute in boiling water. Refresh under cold water and drain.
5. To serve, arrange vegetables on a platter according to color and place mayonnaise in a hollowed red cabbage.

6–8 portions

Lemon Thyme Mayonnaise

1 egg

1 tablespoon lemon juice

1 lemon rind, grated

1 teaspoon dijon mustard

½ teaspoon salt

2 tablespoons chives and parsley, minced

2 tablespoons lemon thyme, minced

1 cup oil (½ salad oil, ½ olive oil)

1. Combine the egg, lemon juice, lemon rind, mustard, salt, and herbs in a blender and mix for a few seconds.
2. With the motor running, add the oil drop by drop from a baster until about half has been incorporated into the yolk and the mixture has begun to thicken.
3. Slowly add the remaining oil in a stream. Taste for seasoning. Chill.

Yields approximately 1 ¼ cups

Assorted Stuffed Eggs

Herbs and Scallions

4 eggs, hard-boiled, shells removed

1 tablespoon fresh parsley, minced

1 teaspoon fresh tarragon, minced

2 teaspoons fresh chives, minced

1 scallion, minced

2 tablespoons mayonnaise

2 teaspoons dijon mustard

¼ teaspoon salt, freshly ground white pepper

Caviar and Sour Cream

4 eggs, hard-boiled, shells removed

1 tablespoon red caviar

2 tablespoons sour cream

2 tablespoons cream cheese

½ teaspoon lemon juice

¼ teaspoon salt, freshly ground white pepper

In each case, cut the eggs in half lengthwise and remove yolks. Blend the yolks with all the other ingredients in the work bowl of a food processor. Spoon into the egg whites and chill.

8 portions or 16 stuffed eggs

Tom Thumb Cheesecakes

These cheesecakes add just the right touch for the end of the picnic. By dividing the mixture before baking, two different flavors are provided for the kite-fliers. No utensils are needed for eating.

1¾ cups graham cracker crumbs, finely ground

½ teaspoon cinnamon

¼ cup almonds, chopped

½ cup butter, melted

3 eggs, well beaten

1 pound cream cheese, softened

1 cup sugar

¼ teaspoon salt

2 teaspoons vanilla

½ teaspoon almond extract

3 cups sour cream

3 ounces semisweet chocolate, melted

1 tablespoon heavy cream

1 orange rind, grated

⅓ cup almonds, chopped

7 fresh strawberries, sliced

2 tablespoons red currant jelly

extra grated chocolate for garnish

1. Preheat oven to 375°.
2. Combine graham cracker crumbs with cinnamon, almonds, and melted butter. Press a heaping tablespoon into the bottom and sides of 14 4-ounce ramekins that have parchment paper cut to fit the bottoms. Set aside.
3. Combine eggs, cream cheese, sugar, salt, vanilla, and almond extract, beating until smooth. Blend in the sour cream. Divide the mixture in half.
4. Mix the melted chocolate with heavy cream and orange rind, and blend this mixture into one half of the cream cheese mixture. Do not overmix; the chocolate should have a swirled effect. Divide among 7 ramekins.
5. Blend the chopped almonds into the other half of the cream cheese mixture and divide among 7 ramekins.
6. Bake at 375° for about 30 minutes or until set. Cool.
7. Unmold the cheesecakes from the ramekins. Decorate the almond cheesecakes with sliced strawberries; heat the red currant jelly and drizzle over the top. Decorate the swirled chocolate cheesecakes with grated chocolate.

Yields 14 miniature cheesecakes

Crabapple blossoms

End-of-Winter Dinner

Pasta with Country Ham, Snow Peas,
and Asparagus

*   *   *

Roast Leg of Lamb with Braised Scallion Sauce

Sautéed Cherry Tomatoes and Yellow Squash
with Basil Butter

Molded Rice with Spinach and Parmesan Cheese

*   *   *

Chocolate Soufflé with
Chocolate Sauce and Whipped Cream

Serves 6–8 people

Pasta with country ham, snow peas,
and asparagus

Pasta with Country Ham, Snow Peas, and Asparagus

1½ pounds fresh asparagus

8 ounces snow peas

6 ounces country ham, cut into matchstick pieces

1 tablespoon butter

1 cup heavy cream

1 recipe Homemade Pasta

3 ounces parmesan cheese, freshly grated

2 tablespoons fresh parsley, minced

1½ teaspoons tarragon

2 ounces pine nuts, toasted

optional: 18 mussels, cooked in their shells, for garnish

1. Trim and wash asparagus. Bring water to a boil in a saucepan and cook the asparagus for 2–3 minutes until tender but still firm. Drain and refresh under cold water to set the bright green color. Snap off the tips, cut the stalks into ¾″ pieces, and set aside.
2. String the snow peas from each end. Cook in boiling water for 30–60 seconds, drain, and refresh with cold water. Cut into diagonal pieces and set aside.
3. Sauté the ham in 1 tablespoon butter over medium low heat for 2–3 minutes. Add the cream and cook over medium high heat for a few minutes until cream thickens.
4. Cook the homemade pasta for 2 minutes until *al dente* (if using commercially prepared pasta, cook according to directions), drain, and transfer to a warmed serving dish. Add the vegetables, ham mixture, cheese, and herbs. Toss and serve immediately. Garnish with pine nuts and mussels. Pass additional cheese.

6–8 portions

Homemade Pasta

Pasta made with 2 eggs, 2 cups of flour, a pinch of salt, and a teaspoon of olive oil is a sufficient amount for a first course for 6 people. The same proportions will feed 2 people as a main course.

The roast should be removed from the oven when the internal temperature reads 165°. It will continue to cook for a few minutes after it comes from the oven, and the temperature will continue to rise.

Roast Leg of Lamb with Braised Scallion Sauce

1 leg of lamb, about 8 pounds, boned

4 lemon rinds, chopped

10 garlic cloves, chopped

4 lemons, juiced

1 teaspoon salt

3 teaspoons pepper, freshly ground

½ bunch parsley, chopped

2 teaspoons fresh rosemary, chopped

1 teaspoon fresh thyme, chopped

½ cup olive oil

1 recipe Braised Scallion Sauce

1. Mix the chopped lemon rind, lemon juice, garlic, salt, pepper, herbs, and oil. Marinate the lamb in this mixture for 24 hours.
2. Preheat oven to 375°.
3. Roll and tie the marinated lamb. Coat outside with the remaining marinade.
4. Roast uncovered, fat side up, on a rack at 375° for 20 minutes per pound. Cook until instant thermometer reads 165°; remove from oven.
5. Serve sliced with scallion sauce; top each serving with 2–3 scallions.

6 portions

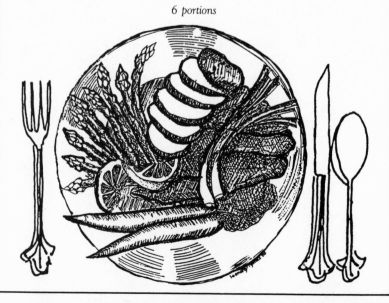

Braised Scallion Sauce

18 scallions

1 tablespoon butter

1½ cups chicken stock

3 tablespoons sugar

¼ teaspoon salt, freshly
   ground white pepper

½ cup heavy cream

2 tablespoons dijon mustard

1. Wash and clean the scallions and trim the tops off, leaving about
   1″ of green showing.
2. Melt butter in a heavy skillet and add chicken stock and sugar.
   Bring to a boil and add scallions, salt, and pepper. Cook partially covered over medium low heat until scallions can be
   pierced with a fork. Remove from pan and set aside.
3. Raise heat in skillet to slightly reduce liquid. Add heavy cream
   and mustard. Simmer and stir until sauce is smooth and slightly
   reduced. Add scallions to the pan to warm.

6 portions

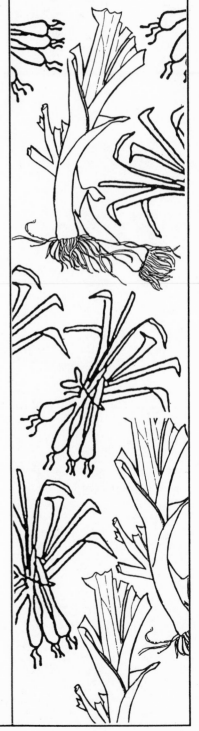

*Variations: Leeks braised
in the same butter, chicken
stock, and sugar are a delightful accompaniment to
steaks or other red meats.
Sprinkle lightly with freshly
grated parmesan cheese as
they are served.*

Sautéed Cherry Tomatoes and Yellow Squash with Basil Butter

8 ounces yellow squash

16 ounces cherry tomatoes

2 tablespoons Basil Butter (recipe p. 136)

¼ teaspoon salt, freshly ground pepper

Cut the squash into pieces roughly the size of the cherry tomatoes. Melt the basil butter in a large skillet and cook the squash for 8–10 minutes until crispy tender. Add the cherry tomatoes and cook for an additional 2 minutes. Season with salt and pepper.

6 portions

Molded Rice with Spinach and Parmesan Cheese

2 cups water

1 cup rice

4 ounces fresh spinach or Swiss chard

4 tablespoons fresh parsley, minced

½ teaspoon salt, freshly ground pepper

freshly grated nutmeg

2 tablespoons heavy cream

1½ ounces parmesan cheese, freshly grated

1 carrot, cooked, notched lengthwise, and sliced crosswise into flower shapes

1. Bring water to a boil, add rice, and simmer covered for about 16–18 minutes.
2. Wash spinach and remove the center rib. Wilt spinach in a skillet, using only the water clinging to the leaves from washing. Cool and squeeze by the handful to remove any remaining water. Finely chop the spinach and parsley together. Blend with the salt, pepper, nutmeg, and heavy cream. Add along with parmesan to the rice.
3. To serve, pack into individual molds with a carrot slice in the bottom. Leave in molds for 3 minutes, invert onto plate, and tap the side of the mold to help it release.

6 portions

Chocolate Soufflé with Chocolate Sauce and Whipped Cream

3 tablespoons unsalted butter

1 tablespoon flour

1 cup milk

6 tablespoons sugar

2 teaspoons vanilla

pinch of salt

8 ounces unsweetened chocolate

12 egg whites

½ teaspoon cream of tartar

confectioners' sugar

1 recipe Chocolate Soufflé Sauce

½ pint heavy cream, whipped and sweetened

1. Preheat oven to 400°.
2. Melt butter, add flour, and cook over medium heat for 2–3 minutes, stirring constantly. Heat milk and add it all at once, whisking rapidly. Add sugar, vanilla, and salt.
3. Melt chocolate over the lowest setting possible, cool slightly, and blend with the milk mixture.
4. Beat egg whites until they are foamy. Add cream of tartar and continue beating until they hold stiff peaks. Fold the whites into the chocolate mixture.
5. Butter six 8-ounce ramekins and fill each ⅔ full with the soufflé mixture. Bake at 400° for 8–10 minutes. Dust the tops of the soufflé with confectioners' sugar. Serve immediately with a small pitcher of chocolate soufflé sauce and whipped cream.

6 portions

Edna Lewis, one of America's foremost authorities on Southern food, spent almost a full year as a guest chef at Fearrington House. She is the author of two cookbooks that weave history and tradition with food.

This recipe is our adaptation of the chocolate soufflé made famous by Ms. Lewis. It differs from the original in sweetness and in the thickness of the chocolate sauce.

If the base of the soufflé should curdle after blending it with the milk, beat in warm half-and-half by the tablespoon until the mixture becomes smooth.

Chocolate Soufflé Sauce

**4 ounces unsweetened chocolate,
cut into pieces**

1 cup sugar

⅛ teaspoon salt

¾ cup heavy cream

¼ cup half-and-half

1 teaspoon vanilla

1. Melt the chocolate in a heavy-bottomed saucepan over very low heat. Remove from heat and add sugar and salt. Heat cream and half-and-half until just under a boil. Slowly add to the chocolate mixture, stirring constantly.
2. Return the chocolate mixture to the stove and heat gently until completely smooth, stirring constantly. Remove from heat and add vanilla. Cool to room temperature. Adjust consistency with additional cream if necessary. This sauce can be stored in the refrigerator for several days. Reheat in a double boiler.

Yields approximately 2 cups

Winter Projects

1. Planting the Wildflower Field

2. Forcing Blossoms

3. Planting Paper-whites

Planting the Wildflower Field

Seed for flowers for meadow gardening is now readily available in many different stores, some of which sell mixtures that are regionally blended. The selection should contain perennials and self-seeding annuals.

A blend should contain flowers such as bachelor's buttons, coreopsis, black-eyed Susans, gaillardia, oxeye daisy, chicory, and Queen Anne's Lace among its offerings, for these particular wildflowers bloom all over the United States. If one likes to garden, it can be an interesting project to find native plants that can naturalize and spread. Most selections also have flowers that will show some color in succession from spring until fall.

Select the area to be planted in the fall and turn the soil at that time. Be certain there is good drainage; add humus if the soil is poor.

The seeds should be in the ground by mid-March. To plant, mix the seeds with sand and broadcast them evenly over the area. One pound of seeds should cover 1,000 square feet. Press the seeds into the ground and cover lightly with soil and/or pine straw. The birds will find seeds and eat them if the planted area is not properly covered.

Meadow gardening reduces maintenance of areas that are unattractive. Weed control is still a problem until fields are well established, however. If annual seeds alone are planted, the field will have a bloom span of three weeks and then revert to weeds. The weeding is hard work, but a spectacular meadow garden in bloom is well worth the effort.

At Fearrington we reseed our meadow garden each season. We gather seed at the proper time, clean it, label it, store it for the winter, and plant it in February or early March. Often we transfer plants to the field to help create a mass effect with favorite flowers. We fertilize in the spring, water if rainfall is inadequate, and mow in the late fall to help control weeds and redistribute seeds.

When the garden blooms, the color is breathtaking.

INDEX

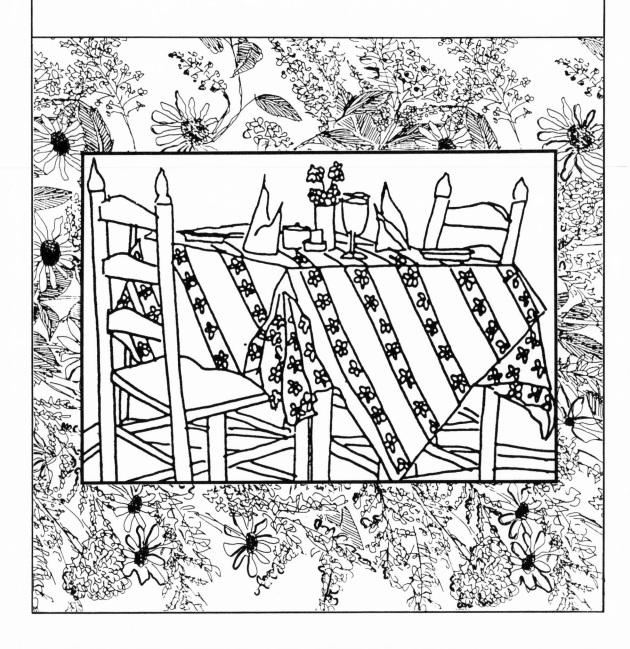

Index

A

Acorn squash, *see* Squash
After the Game menu, 141
Afternoon Tea menu, 187
Almonds:
  almond crescent cookies, 192
  almond crisp cookies, 94
  almond praline, 94
  with lemon rice, 83
Amaretto truffles, 174
Angel biscuits with honeycup
  mustard and country ham, 49
Apple tart, country, 155
Apricot walnut dressing, 178
Artichokes:
  artichoke-asparagus vinaigrette,
  24
  with matchstick vegetables, 208
  with pasta, country ham, and
  snow peas, 251
Asparagus:
  artichoke-asparagus vinaigrette,
  23
  steamed, with snow peas, 18
  vinaigrette, 33
August Ice Cream Party menu, 87
Autumn flower arrangements,
  144, 146, 156, 171, 177,
  181, 189

B

Baked beans, 153
Baked cherry tomatoes with
  toasted bread crumbs, 44
Baked mushrooms stuffed with
  country sausage, 50
Baked stuffed squash, 107
Banana fritters, 237
Banana ice cream, 89
Barbeque, instructions for, 151
Barbeque menu, 149
Barbeque sauce, Robert's, 152
Basic butter cookies, 93
Basil:
  basil-garlic vinegar, 135
  butter, 136
  harvesting, 129
  pesto sauce, 138
  sorbet, 98
Beans:
  baked, 153
  French green, 182
  green, and okra in vinaigrette,
  80

green, and potato salad, 108
green, with fines herbes butter,
  43
green and wax, with bread
  crumbs, 146
Beef, *see* Roasts
Beets, pickled, 184
Bell peppers, *see* Peppers
Berrypatch champagne, 41
Beverages:
  berrypatch champagne, 41
  Bloody Lucy, 13
  cranberry raspberry kir, 203
  Fearrington House cooler, 97
  lemon balm cooler, 77
  May wine, 23
Biscuits:
  angel, with honeycup mustard
  and country ham, 49
  herbed, 215
  miniature, with country ham,
  215
  sausage pinwheel, 36
  Southern biscuit muffins, 111
Black walnut chocolate pound
  cake, 189
Blackberry ice cream with
  candied lemon peel, 91
Blackberry sauce, 46, 104
Black-eyed peas:
  Hoppin' John, 227
  summer salad, 110
  with rosemary, 234
  with Vidalia onion cups, 158
Bloody Lucy, 13
Blueberry sauce, 46
Borage:
  blossoms, with cucumber soup,
  41
  harvesting, 129
Bouquet garni (project), 196
Bourbon balls, 230
Bourbon pecan pie, Fearrington
  House, 148
Braised scallion sauce, 253
Bread:
  braided bread ring, 69
  hush puppies, 154
  monkey bread, 165
  picnic basket bread, 122
  scones, 190
  spoonbread with country ham,
  228
  see also Biscuits, Muffins

Bride's bouquet (project), 60
Bridesmaids' Luncheon menu, 39
Broccoli with sesame seeds, 234
Brunch, Easter, menu, 11
Brunswick stew, 152
Brussels sprouts and leeks, 183
Butter:
  basil, 136
  chive, 136
  fines herbes, 136
  green peppercorn, 137
  lemon, 18
  lemon herb, 137
  lemon thyme, 101
  tarragon, 36, 137
Butter cookies, basic, 93

C

Cabbage:
  slaw, 154
  with bacon and croutons, 184
Cake:
  black walnut chocolate pound,
  189
  chocolate cheesecake, with
  raspberry sauce, 169
  coconut, 210
  orange date, 70
  Tom Thumb cheesecake, 247
Candied grapefruit peel, 173
Candied lemon peel, 91
Candied orange peel, 173
Candied violets, 63, 70
Caramelizing syrup, 85
Carrots:
  baby, glazed, 35
  carrot soup with bacon and
  orange peel, 177
  fines herbes, 29
  glazed, with turnips and
  chestnuts, 219
  steamed, with celery, 164
  with smooth tomato dressing,
  117
Cassis ice cubes, 215
Celebration of Fall menu, 157
Champagne, berrypatch, 41
Cheese:
  cheddar cheese pastry, 53
  cream cheese pastry, 148
  goat cheese tart, 241
  herbed, in braided bread ring,
  69
  herbed, Joaquin's, 121

pimiento, 123
soufflé, twice-baked, 34
straws, pecan date, 192
wafers with pecans, 72
white cheddar, with squash gratin, 102
Cheesecake:
chocolate, with raspberry sauce, 169
Tom Thumb cheesecakes, 247
Cherry tomatoes, 44, 254
Chestnuts, glazed, with carrots and turnips, 219
Chicken:
Chicken Country Captain, 235
chicken pot pie, 233
chicken salad, with oranges and toasted almonds, 43
with lemon parsley sauce, 24
Chili, 226
Chilled cucumber soup with borage blossoms, 41
Chilled tomato soup with basil sorbet, 97
Chilled vegetables with lemon thyme mayonnaise, 245
Chives:
chive blossom vinegar, 135
chive butter, 136
dill chive sauce, 51
harvesting, 129
tarragon-chive mayonnaise, 79
Chocolate:
cheesecake, with raspberry sauce, 169
coffee sauce, 90
curls, 166
ice cream, 30, 89
leaves, 172
roulade, with coffee ice cream and Kahlua sauce, 170
sauce, Lucinda's, 90
soufflé, with chocolate sauce and whipped cream, 255
soufflé sauce, 256
tulip shells, 20
Christmas Dinner menu, 201
Cinnamon-nutmeg ice cream, 113
Cobbler, peach, 112
Coconut cake, 210
Coffee ice cream, 171
Coffee punch, 74
Coleslaw, 154
Confetti rice, 206
Cookies:
almond crescent, 192
almond crisps, 94
basic butter, 93
fruitcake, miniature, 209
icebox, 86
macaroons, 71
see also Scones

Coolers:
Fearrington House, 97
lemon balm, 77
Corn chowder with red bell peppers, 234
Corn soufflé with sweet golden peppers, 179
Cornbread muffins with bacon, 84
Cornmeal crepes with country ham and leeks, 13–14
Country apple tart with lemon zest and vanilla ice cream, 155
Country ham:
how to prepare, 178
with angel biscuits and honey-cup mustard, 49
with cornmeal crepes and leeks, 13
with crabmeat (appetizer), 204
with miniature biscuits, 215
with pasta, snow peas, and asparagus, 251
with spoonbread, 228
Crab:
cakes, with tarragon-chive mayonnaise, 78
quiche, 52
ramekin, 15
with country ham (appetizer), 204
Cranberry raspberry kir, 203
Cream of Vidalia onion soup, 143
Creasie green soup, 161
Crepes, cornmeal, 13–14
Croutons, 184
Cucumber dill mayonnaise, 6
Cucumber sandwiches, 54
Cucumber soup with borage blossoms, 41

D
Dessert after the Symphony menu, 167
Dill:
cucumber dill mayonnaise, 6
dill chive sauce, 51
harvesting, 129
Double pie crust, 9
Dressing:
apricot walnut, 178
smooth tomato, 117
Drying flowers and weeds (project), 132

E
Early March Kite Flying menu, 239
Easter Brunch menu, 11
Eggplant and zucchini stuffed with rice and tomatoes, 164
Eggs, assorted stuffed, 246
End-of-Winter Dinner menu, 249

F
Fall, see Autumn
Fearrington House bourbon pecan pie, 148
Fearrington House Chicken Country Captain, 235
Fearrington House cooler, 97
Fearrington House fruit punch, 56
Fines herbes, with carrots, 29
Fines herbes butter, 136
First Day of Spring menu, 3
Fish dishes:
poached salmon with cucumber dill mayonnaise, 6
red snapper with matchstick vegetables, 81
Flowers:
building an arrangement, 17
cutting and conditioning, 78–79
drying, 132–34
edible, 102–3
for bride's bouquet, 61
forcing, 260
planting, 259, 261
tips for arranging, 22, 51, 71, 78–79, 226, 227
for seasonal arrangements, see under Spring, Summer, Autumn, Winter
Forcing blossoms (project), 260
French green beans, 182
Fresh coconut cake with rum and orange filling, 210
Fresh fruit with Grand Marnier sauce, 124
Fresh pumpkin pie with ginger whipped cream, 185
Fresh tomato tart, 42
Fried green tomatoes, 109
Fritters, banana, 237
Fruit:
fresh, in watermelon basket, 70
fresh, with grand Marnier sauce, 124
punch, Fearrington House, 56
Fruitcake cookies, miniature, 209

G
Garden Harvest Dinner menu, 105
Garden party topiary, 59
Garden peas with tarragon butter, 36
Garlic:
basil-garlic olive oil, 135
basil-garlic vinegar, 135
mayonnaise, 83
Gazpacho molded timbale, 17
Ginger whipped cream, 185
Glazed baby carrots, 35

Glazed carrots, turnips, and chestnuts, 219
Goat cheese tart, 241
Graduation Dinner menu, 21
Grand Marnier:
  chocolate sauce, 90
  sauce, 125
  sherbet with orange mint nougatine, 85
Grapefruit peel, candied, 173
Grapefruit vodka sorbet, 218
Grapevine wreath with flowers, 244
Grated sweet potato pudding, 180
Gratin of leeks and spring onions, 5
Gratin of squash with white cheddar cheese, 102
Green beans, see Beans
Green peppercorn butter, 137
Green peppercorn sauce, 144
Greens, sautéed baby, 8
Grits timbale, 145
Groundhog Day Lunch menu, 231

H

Ham, see Country ham
Harvesting herbs (project),
Hazelnut meringue shells, 30
Heart-shaped scones with currants, 190
Hearty vegetable soup, 225
Herbs:
  chopped, 108
  harvesting, 129–31
  herb butters, 136–37
  herb swag, 207
  herb vinegars and oils, 135
  herb wreath (project), 195
  herbed cheese, Joaquin's, 121
Honey lemon vinaigrette, 32
Honeymoon basket, 62
Hoppin' John, 227
Hush puppies, 154

I

Icebox cookies, 86
Ice cream:
  banana, 89
  blackberry, 91
  chocolate, 30, 89
  cinnamon-nutmeg, 113
  coffee, 171
  lemon, 92
  peach, 89
  peppermint, 89
  vanilla, 89
Ice cream, toppings for, 93
Ice Cream Party menu, 87

K

Kahlua sauce, 170

L

Labor Day Picnic menu, 115
Lamb, roast leg of, with braised scallion sauce, 252
Leeks:
  good with red meat, 253
  gratin of, and spring onions, 5
  onion, leek, and shallot tart, 118
  with Brussels sprouts, 183
  with ham and cornmeal crepes, 13
  with Vidalia onions in vinaigrette, 25
Lemon:
  butter, 18, 137
  candied peel, 91
  curd, 104
  honey lemon vinaigrette, 32
  ice cream, with strawberry sauce, 92
  lemon balm cooler, 77
  lemon chess tart, 229
  lemon frost pie, with blueberry sauce, 45
  lemon parsley sauce, 26
  lemon rice with almonds, 83
  Lemon Shaker Pie, 9
  lemon thyme butter, 101
  lemon thyme mayonnaise, 245
Lentil salad, 119

M

Macaroons, 71
May wine, 23
Mayonnaise:
  cucumber dill, 6
  garlic, 83
  lemon thyme, 245
  red bell pepper, 160
  tarragon-chive, 79
Meringue:
  hazelnut shells, 30
  miniature shells, 55
Miniature biscuits with country ham, 215
Miniature bran muffins, 73
Miniature fruitcake cookies, 209
Miniature glazed orange muffins, 191
Miniature meringue shells with glazed strawberries, 55
Mint:
  harvesting, 130
  orange mint nougatine, 85
Molded gazpacho timbale, 17
Monkey bread, 165
Mornay sauce, 14
Morning Coffee menu, 67
Mother's Day Lunch menu, 31
Muffins:
  cornbread, with bacon, 84
  miniature bran, 73
  miniature fruitcake, 209

miniature glazed orange, 191
Southern biscuit, 111
Mushrooms:
  baked, stuffed with country sausage, 50
  mushroom roll, with red bell pepper mayonnaise, 159
  mushroom sausage tart, 120
  mushroom spinach timbale, 27
  sautéed button mushrooms with brandy, 147
Mussel soup with red pepper cream, 216

N

New Year's Eve menu, 213

O

Okra and green beans vinaigrette, 80
Olive oil, basil-garlic, 135
Onions:
  baked Vidalia, 165
  cream of Vidalia onion soup, 143
  onion, leek, and shallot tart, 118
  spring, gratin of, with leeks, 5
  Vidalia, and leeks vinaigrette, 26
  Vidalia onion cups with black-eyed peas, 158
Orange:
  candied peel, 173
  filling for cake, 210
  glaze, 191
  orange date cake, with whipped cream and candied violets, 70
  orange mint ice cream, 85
  orange muffins, miniature glazed, 191
  orange pastry shell, 222
  orange saffron rice, 8
  orange tomato juice, 69
  sauce, 237
Oysters, scalloped, 236

P

Paper-white narcissus (project), 261
Parsley:
  harvesting, 130
  lemon parsley sauce, 26
Pasta:
  homemade, 251
  salad, with pine nuts and pesto, 243
  salad, Walter's, 244
  with vegetables and country ham, 251
Pastry:
  all-purpose, 53

cheddar cheese, 53
cream cheese, 148
double, 9
for goat cheese tart, 242
herbed, 53
never-fail, 100
orange, 222
partially baked, 100
pot pie, 233
scallop pastry shells, 100
Peach cobbler with cinnamon-
nutmeg ice cream, 112
Peach ice cream, 89
Pears, poached, with raspberry
sauce and chocolate curls,
166
Peas, garden, with tarragon
butter, 36
see also Black-eyed peas, Snow
peas, Sugar snap peas
Pecans:
bourbon pecan pie, 148
pecan date cheese straws, 192
with cheese wafers, 72
with Swiss chard, 163
Peppercorn sauce, 144
Peppermint ice cream, 89
Peppers:
golden, with corn soufflé, 179
red bell, with corn chowder,
234
red bell, with lentil salad,
119
red bell pepper cream, 217
red bell pepper mayonnaise,
160
roasted, 217
Persimmon chiffon pie, 186
Pesto sauce, 138
Pickled beets, 184
Picnic, Labor Day, menu, 115
Picnic basket bread, 122
Pie:
bourbon pecan, 148
chicken pot, 233
lemon chess, 229
lemon frost, with blueberry
sauce, 45
persimmon chiffon, 186
pumpkin, 185
Shaker Lemon, 9
see also Tart
Pie crust, see Pastry
Pig Pickin' in the Barn menu,
149
Pimiento cheese, 123
Planting paper-whites (project),
261
Planting the wildflower field
(project), 259
Poached pears with raspberry
sauce and chocolate curls,
166

Poached salmon with cucumber
dill mayonnaise, 6
Pork, medallions of, 162
Potatoes:
new, in their jackets, 8
potato salad, Tina's, with green
beans and bacon, 108
skillet, with scallions and
chives, 153
sweet potato pudding, 180
Potpourri (project), 197
Praline, almond, 94
Pudding, sweet potato, 180
Pumpkin pie, 185
Punch:
coffee, 74
fruit, Fearrington House, 56

Q

Quiche, crab, 52

R

Ramekin, crab, 15
Raspberry sauce, 46, 166, 169
Raspberry sorbet in chocolate
tulip shells, 19
Rice:
confetti, 206
Hoppin' John, 227
lemon, with almonds, 83
molded, with spinach and
parmesan cheese, 254
orange saffron, 7
with scallions and chives, 220
with shallots and poppy seeds,
28
with tomatoes, eggplant, and
zucchini, 164
Roasts:
leg of lamb, with braised
scallion sauce, 252
roasting time for beef, 205
standing rib, 205
tenderloin of beef, with
Madeira sauce, 218
veal loin roast, 162
Roll, mushroom, 159
Rosemary:
harvesting, 131
with black-eyed peas, 234
Roulade, chocolate, 170

S

Saffron rice, orange, 7
Salad:
carrot, 117
chicken, with oranges and
toasted almonds, 43
lentil, with sweet red bell
peppers, 119
pasta, Walter's, 244
pasta, with pine nuts and
pesto, 243

potato, Tina's, with green
beans and bacon, 108
summer black-eyed pea, 110
Salmon, poached, with cucumber
dill mayonnaise, 6
Sauce:
barbeque, Robert's, 152
Beaujolais, 205
blackberry, 46, 104
blueberry, 46
braised scallion, 253
chocolate, Lucinda's, 90
chocolate coffee, 90
chocolate soufflé, 256
dill chive, 51
Grand Marnier, 125
Grand Marnier chocolate, 90
green peppercorn, 144
Kahlua, 170
lemon parsley, 26
Madeira, 218
Mornay, 14
orange, 237
pesto, 138
raspberry, 46, 166, 169
strawberry, 93
Sausage:
mushroom sausage tart, 120
mushrooms stuffed with, 50
sausage pinwheel biscuits, 36
Sautéed baby greens, 8
Sautéed button mushrooms with
brandy, 147
Sautéed cherry tomatoes and
yellow squash with basil
butter, 254
Scallion sauce, braised, 253
Scallops and shrimp in scallop
pastry shells, 99
Scones, heart-shaped, with
currants, 190
Seafood Dinner menu, 75
Shaker Lemon Pie, 9
Shallots:
onion, leek, and shallot tart,
118
with rice and poppy seeds, 28
Sherbet, Grand Marnier, with
orange mint nougatine, 85
Shortbread, with lemon curd and
blackberry sauce, 103
Shortcake, strawberry, 37
Shrimp, instructions for cooking,
81
Shrimp and scallops in scallop
pastry shells, 99
Slaw, 154
Snapper, red, with vegetables,
81
Snow peas:
steamed, with asparagus, 18
with pasta, country ham, and
asparagus, 251

with sugar snaps, in lemon thyme butter, 101
Sorbet:
    basil, 98
    pink grapefruit vodka, 218
    raspberry, 19
Soufflé:
    chocolate, 255
    corn, with sweet golden peppers, 179
    spinach, 220
    twice-baked cheese, 34
Soup:
    carrot, with bacon and orange peel, 177
    corn chowder, 234
    cream of Vidalia onion, 143
    creasie green, 161
    cucumber, with borage blossoms, 41
    hearty vegetable, 225
    mussel, with red pepper cream, 216
    tomato, with basil sorbet, 97
Southern biscuit muffins, 111
Spinach:
    mushroom spinach timbale, 27
    soufflé, with acorn squash, 220
    with baked acorn squash and pine nuts, 181
    with rice and parmesan cheese, 254
Spoonbread with country ham, 228
Spring flower arrangements, 5, 7, 12, 16–17, 18, 38, 48
Squash:
    acorn, baked, with spinach and pine nuts, 181
    acorn, with spinach soufflé, 220
    baked stuffed, 107
    gratin, with white cheddar cheese, 102
    yellow, with cherry tomatoes and basil butter, 254
Steamed asparagus and snow peas with lemon butter, 18
Stew, Brunswick, 152
Strawberries:
    glazed, 55
    strawberry sauce, 93
    strawberry shortcake, 37
Stuffed eggs, 246
Sugar snap peas, 101
Sugarplums, 225
Summer black-eyed pea salad, 110
Summer Evening with Music menu, 95
Summer flower arrangements, 83, 91, 101, 109, 111, 117, 121, 123, 125

Summer Seafood Dinner menu, 75
Sweet potato pudding, 180
Sweet red bell peppers with lentil salad, 119
Swiss chard with pecans, 163

T

Tarragon:
    butter, 36, 137
    harvesting, 131
    tarragon-chive mayonnaise, 79
    vinegar, 135
Tart:
    country apple, 155
    goat cheese, 241
    lemon chess, 229
    mushroom sausage, 120
    onion, leek, and shallot, 118
    tomato, 42
    walnut lace, 221
    see also Pie
Tea in the Afternoon menu, 187
Thanksgiving Day menu, 175
Timbale:
    grits, 145
    molded gazpacho, 17
    mushroom spinach, 27
Tomatoes:
    as shells for stuffing, 164
    cherry, baked, with toasted bread crumbs, 44
    cherry, sautéed, with yellow squash and basil butter, 254
    green, fried, 109
    tomato dressing, 117
    tomato soup, with basil sorbet, 97
    tomato tart, 42
Tom Thumb cheesecakes, 247
Topiary, 59
Truffles, amaretto, 174
Turnips, glazed, with carrots and chestnuts, 219
Twice-baked cheese soufflé, 34

V

Vanilla ice cream, 89
Veal:
    loin roast, 162
    saddle of, stuffed with veal tenderloin, 24
Vegetables:
    chilled, with lemon thyme mayonnaise, 245
    hearty vegetable soup, 225
    matchstick, 81, 208
Vidalia onions, see Onions
Vinaigrette, 33, 244
Vinegars, herb, 135
Violets, candied, 63

W

Walnut lace tart, 221
Watermelon basket, fresh fruit in, 70
Wax beans and green beans with bread crumbs, 146
Wedding:
    bride's bouquet for (project), 60
    honeymoon basket for (project), 62
    topiary for (project), 59
Wedding Reception menu, 47
Weeds, drying (project), 132
Wildflower field, 91, 259
Winter flower arrangements, 206, 216, 230, 236, 241, 242, 244
Winter Get-Together menu, 223
Wreath:
    grapevine, with flowers, 244
    herb (project), 195

Z

Zucchini, with eggplant, 164

About the Author

Jenny Fitch is a native of North Carolina and a graduate of the University of North Carolina at Chapel Hill. For eight years, while raising her family, she studied French cooking and since then has attended cooking schools both in the United States and abroad. Instrumental in converting Fearrington House from a farmhouse to a restaurant, she was executive chef in the early years and still works with the staff in menu selection. As its owner, she oversees the gardens, does flowers for the restaurant and inn, and is responsible for the interior design and ambiance of the restaurant.